Foreword by Lord Provost Susan Baird

1990 promises to be the high point of a remarkable decade which has seen the fortunes of Glasgow transformed. It has been a tremendous privilege for me to have been a member of the Council which has played a key role in the renaissance of this great city.

I was elected Lord Provost just weeks after the Glasgow Garden Festival was officially opened and like everyone who visited that great event I have many happy memories. Now as we move towards lifting the curtain on the Cultural Capital of Europe all of us can sense an air of excitement and expectation.

It will be a truly memorable year during which we will see the opening of the splendid new Glasgow International Concert Hall. This imposing building will be the perfect home for a host of major events from classical concerts to pop concerts, from serious conferences to snooker contests.

The city's civic entrepreneurs have been instrumental in the revival of Glasgow's fortunes through planning, pump-priming and partnership.

The Concert Hall project is part of an inner city renewal born of the city's belief in itself.

Glasgow has established during the past decade a reputation of energetic and innovative approaches to regeneration, substantially based on improving the environment and by promoting tourism and the arts.

The most visible tokens of this have been the Glasgow's Miles Better campaign, the selection by the Government to be host to the 1988 National Garden Festival and the designation by the European Community as Cultural Capital of Europe 1990.

But things go back longer than just ten years. The Council's museums and galleries service has long been regarded as one of the finest in Britain and certainly no visit to the city can be complete without a tour of the magnificent Burrell Collection.

There, a breathtaking array of artefacts from the ancient world, oriental art, medieval tapestries, paintings and much more are displayed in an award-winning gallery in the heart of the heavily wooded Pollok Country Park.

Glasgow is the home of most of Scotland's national performing arts organizations, and has nine major theatres and performance spaces. Annual events include Mayfest, an international springtime celebration of popular visual and performing arts.

It is this rich and vibrant cultural life which led to Glasgow being accorded the accolade Cultural Capital of Europe for 1990.

Everyone has worked so hard to make 1990 a year in which Glasgow performs on the world stage. There will be lots to see and do for both resident and visitor alike. I know that 1990 will indeed be a year to remember.

A Message of Welcome by Councillor James Jennings, Convenor of Strathclyde Regional Council

It's no coincidence that Glasgow's renaissance has taken place in the lifetime of Strathclyde. When the Regional Council was set up fifteen years ago, it insisted on the need for a strong heart if the whole region was to gain vitality.

Using its powers as the biggest local authority in the country, the Council set about redirecting its resources to tackle the problems of the areas which had suffered most from the decline of traditional industry – and most of them lay within the city.

It prepared the ground for new development by providing the necessary infrastructure of roads and water supplies and all the hidden services which people take for granted.

And it used its strong voice to argue, not only for incoming industry, but also for events which would bring visitors to the city and region.

Strathclyde Regional Council has made – and is still making – its contribution to the Burrell Collection. It is investing in the new Concert Hall and the extended McLellan Galleries. It is putting money into the conversion of the Old Atheneum and the expanded Glasgow Film Theatre.

And the council has been a leader in attracting major conferences and conventions to the city – and making sure that visitors enjoy themselves so much that they want to come back.

That's why we're so delighted to be playing our part in the 1990 celebrations, sometimes in partnership with the District Council, sometimes on our own.

1990 offers a marvellous chance for all our citizens to share in a feast of culture. There's something on the menu to suit all tastes: what's more important, there are plenty of chances for people to get involved, whether they live in the city or in the surrounding region.

But the year of culture is also an opportunity for people from outside to get to know us and what we have to offer.

We look forward to welcoming a variety of visitors in the coming year.

There will be artists from all over the world who are coming to share their skills and set international standards.

There will be the people who come in their train — the support staff, the dignatories, and, of course, the fans who follow their favourite players wherever they are performing.

And we'll be extending an extra-special welcome to the thousands of mentally handicapped athletes and their helpers who will be coming to take part in the European Special Olympics in July. It was the Regional Council which invited them to come and will be looking after them while they are here, so we can take particular pride in the biggest single event of 1990.

We hope that among all these visitors will be some of those who can take decisions on where to place a factory or hold a convention. But we also hope that individuals and families who are attracted by the big names will stay around to get the flavour of Strathclyde, and choose to come back as ordinary tourists.

On behalf of Strathclyde Regional Council, I'd like to extend the old Gaelic greeting of *ceud mille failte* — a hundred thousand welcomes. And I'll finish with another traditional Scottish wish — *Haste Ye Back!*

A Year to Remember by Councillor Pat Lally, Leader of Glasgow District Council

My Council is determined that 1990 will be a year to remember for all Glaswegians.

It will be a year of fun and entertainment with something to suit all tastes.

In our preparation we have striven to ensure that all groups and all cultures within the city are catered for.

Although we want to attract thousands of tourists and visitors whose spending power will bolster the city's economy, 1990 is primarily a festival for local people.

But how did Glasgow manage to achieve the accolade of Cultural Capital of Europe 1990 following in the footsteps of Athens, Florence, Amsterdam, Berlin and Paris?

It took a lot of hard work, determination and confidence back in 1986 to convince Mr Richard Luce, Minister for the Arts, that Glasgow was ready and capable of taking on the prestigious role of Cultural Capital of Europe.

And it worked!

Despite stiff opposition from eight other cities in the United Kingdom Mr Luce recommended Glasgow and he was supported by the Ministers of Culture from the twelve member states of the European Economic Community.

Since then it has been all systems go to organize a year long festival which will bring to the attention of the world, the culture and character of Glasgow. 1990 will reveal Glasgow as a city of dynamism, charisma, culture and fun.

Glasgow is no stranger to culture but never before have we had the opportunity to show it off to the world in such a vast display.

My Council alone spends more than £18 million a year on the visual and performing arts and the city is home to the Scottish National Orchestra, Scottish Opera, the Scottish Ballet and the Royal Scottish Academy of Music and Drama.

There are more than 350 organizations involved in the arts in Glasgow and with their support and the support of both the private and public sectors we are set to stage the greatest show on earth.

There will be an array of international and home-grown talent, casts of thousands, world-class exhibitions and sporting championships. Culture is not just about theatre, dance and music. It is also about sport, art, history and a whole lot more.

The 365-day programme will cover every aspect of culture through almost 2000 events – from world premières in dance, opera and music to more than 400 community events.

My Council has specially commissioned thirty major new works by leading playwrights, choreographers, artists and sculptors.

World-class visiting orchestras will perform in Glasgow's new International Concert Hall which will open on 8 October 1990.

The refurbishment of the McLellan Gallery to the tune of almost £4 million will ensure that it rivals London's Hayward Gallery for facilities and visitor appeal.

More than 125 exhibitions will be held during the year with a series of festivals to celebrate and highlight specific areas of culture.

We will make sure THERE'S A LOT GLASGOWING ON IN 1990 and that the people of Glasgow reap the benefits not only from the enjoyment of the programme but from the many job opportunities that it creates and the amount of money that it generates.

Let's ring up the curtain on Glasgow 1990 – Cultural Capital of Europe.

Joining the Celebration by Councillor Charles Gray, Leader of Strathclyde Regional Council

It's not just the Glasgow folk who are set to enjoy themselves in 1990. The whole of Strathclyde is ready to join in the celebrations, with the full backing of the regional Council.

We see this as a marvellous opportunity to involve everyone in the region, especially those who normally miss out on arts activities. So we've been particularly pleased to work along with Glasgow District Council in planning a year to remember.

As partners in bringing many of the world-class visitors to the city, we've been able to make sure that it's not just the well-heeled and able-bodied who can share in the excitement. And through our own services, we're taking the arts to the parts not covered by the main programme.

So all our schools, colleges and community centres have been encouraged to use the year of culture 1990 as a time to develop new interests and skills, to share their talents with others, and to set up schemes for the future. We want to see 1990 as the base for a much livelier cultural life throughout the region – with the spin-off in training and job opportunities that implies.

For those who have contact with our Social Work Department, too, this year offers a chance to find new confidence and fulfilment through music, dance, painting and drama. Arts venues are being opened up to people with limited mobility and hearing, old folk are seeing their memories recreated through drama, mentally handicapped adults are discovering that they have something to give to others.

And this is going on all round Strathclyde, enriching the lives of our citizens throughout 1990 and for years to come. No wonder the Regional Council is delighted to be a part of it!

so what's all the fuss about?

ROBERT PALMER
FESTIVALS DIRECTOR

Glasgow has always been a city of culture; what's different this year is that the eyes of the world are on us — and on what we're doing to celebrate our designation as European Cultural Capital 1990.

Glasgow has laboured long in the shadows of past difficulties. Now, at last, things are changing for the better. Glasgow's story — from rags to riches, then from turbulent decline to dynamic resurgence — makes the pride we feel in being European Cultural Capital all the more resonant: our struggle has been rewarded, our efforts recognized.

Although sceptics may charge that Glasgow's changes are merely cosmetic and belief in improvement is for those easily gulled by hype generated through advertising and public relations — it's undeniable that there is a widespread perception of the city's renaissance. Not just in Glasgow and Scotland but throughout Britain, Europe and the rest of the world.

Clearly, something meaningful has taken place and is well set to continue. The city has indeed suffered its dark times and painful reminders of those bleak and dreary years have not been completely expunged. But the worst is past and the best is surely still to come.

In the years preceding and following the Second World War, only historians had reason to recall Glasgow's great period as one of the world's wealthiest cities; present miseries proved much too immediate for such indulgence.

'The culture of Glasgow is a culture of character, a culture that lives, works, sings and laughs'.

Yet vast fortunes had been made here — in the tobacco trade, in textiles, in building ships and locomotives. And, if there had only been the opportunity to look and reflect, it would have been apparent that the era when Glasgow was known as the Second City of the Empire had left its mark. And that the city in the twentieth century had inherited some valuable and enduring legacies.

The city could boast a heritage including much magnificent architecture and some of the finest parks in Europe. And it could remember with pride the enlightened thinking that lay behind its pioneering programmes of municipal services; public housing, public water supplies, branch libraries and museums, telephone systems and public baths.

But the depredations of decay were everywhere. The city's neo-classical façades and Victorian renaissance grandeur were lost in the sprawling gray of abandoned warehouses. Deserted quays, rusting cranes and empty shipyards stood as sad monuments to an industrial revolution whose time had passed. In the doldrums of massive unemployment and the severities of poverty, the city could take small consolation in its past glories as a centre for international trade.

Of course this steep decline was not unique: similar stories can be told of all Britain's northern industrial cities. However, Glasgow's story has a special character because of its singular determination to rehabilitate itself.

By no means all its attempts were successful — some were disastrous. Glasgow attacked its grim poverty and over-crowding, believing it could resolve these problems by rehousing its people in new developments ringing the city. The inadequacy of many of these solutions simply perpetuated the problems of poor housing and unemployment. The complexity and intractability of these problems were such that, even today, the damage is still being repaired. But, in recent years, the city's accelerating progress has been remarkable.

Glasgow's spirited revival has had much to do with both its culture of tenacity and the city's tenacious development of its cultural assets. Even within a narrow and extremely conventional definition of culture, the city's resources are considerable.

In the arts alone, no other city outside of London has a comparable array of regularly available theatre, dance and music. There are seventeen major museums, twenty-five art galleries, ten theatres, twelve festivals and two symphony orchestras. And Glasgow is home to almost all Scotland's national performing arts companies — Scottish Opera, the Scottish Ballet, and the Scottish National Orchestra.

The city possesses one of the finest civic art collections — and some of the most fascinating private art collections — in the United Kingdom. The facts speak loudly. The arts sector in Glasgow has a turnover of £300 million each year and employs over sixteen thousand people.

Glasgow is also the centre of Scotland's thriving media industry. And through its two universities, its many colleges, the academy of music and drama and the world famous school of art, Glasgow can justly proclaim itself a city of learning.

But Glasgow's culture is not only conventional, and statistics, while they may impress and beguile, reveal but one small part of the city's cultural strength. The culture of Glasgow is a culture of character, a culture that lives, works, sings and laughs. It's feisty, pawky and ribald, unique in its diversity and range. And the city has not allowed caprices of time and trend to destroy this.

Culture is not only about the arts. Glasgow's culture encompasses all those features which make the city what it is. T. S. Eliot suggested that culture is around us all the time; it envelops just about every human endeavour. Glasgow's culture is in its humour, its street songs, its distinctive patter and its football teams. It's in the dance halls and hairdressing salons, at bus-stops, on its buses and in its pubs. Of course it's also in its opera, ballet, classical music, painting, literature and film. But it's not confined to these things. Lord Raglan is said to have described culture as roughly anything that humans do and monkeys don't. In Glasgow you find people doing just about everything that monkeys don't.

Cultural practices are always subject to choice; and cultural richness depends on the range of available opportunities and options. We must recognize that there are many cultures, and forget obsessions with high and low culture, with elitism and populism. Glasgow's culture is lively, cosmopolitan, and aggressively pluralist.

1990 is really no more of a cultural year than any other. But the city's European status this year has allowed people and groups to take advantage of enhanced opportunities. What has emerged for 1990 is a vast array of projects and events, founded primarily on the best 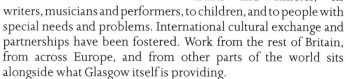 that Glasgow's organizations can offer. In part, the programme represents a contemporary and historical perspective of the city's cultural life and heritage. Consistent encouragement has been given to Glasgow's artists and athletes, its writers, musicians and performers, to children, and to people with special needs and problems. International cultural exchange and partnerships have been fostered. Work from the rest of Britain, from across Europe, and from other parts of the world sits alongside what Glasgow itself is providing.

The emphasis in 1990 is on creation and participation, and on finding new audiences inside the city and across the region. The special cultural projects during 1990 are not there to impose or invade; they surround and inhabit the city, quickening an already lively atmosphere. Many of them may take people by surprise.

Ideas have sprung from the imaginations of more than 450 cultural organizations in Glasgow. In 1990 there is no distinction to separate an official festival from fringe events. This is a people's programme. Something like three thousand people have had a hand in organizing it.

The activities involve every school in Strathclyde. They take place in churches, synagogues and mosques, in hospitals, prisons, residential homes for the elderly and training centres. They happen inside theatres, galleries, universities and community centres; and outside in parks, playing fields, civic squares and in the streets. Most of the time and almost all of the resources have been given to encouraging and helping others, marking a commitment to, and continuing investment in, people, their skills, their vision, aspirations and ambitions.

Such devolution of the programme is deliberate. Commissions

have been placed and new ideas discussed, optimizing opportunities for collaboration and exchange, inviting world famous artists and performers, developing international links, and persuading public and private bodies to offer funds, sponsor events or make services available.

Inevitably, some people will ignore the intentions and look to Glasgow to rival other European arts festivals. Others will concentrate only on miniscule elements of programme planning or specialist interest. They miss the point. 1990 is a means of securing longer term benefits for Glasgow, strengthening infrastructure, extending access, elevating popular and political attitudes to a level where people can see clearly what culture means to the city and imagine practical possibilities for the future. Planners and economists can take comfort in the quantifiable impact of 1990. Positioning Glasgow as a cultural destination for visitors will generate important spin-offs in the hotel, catering and retail sectors servicing Glasgow's market-place for leisure and tourism.

Already in Glasgow over four thousand jobs depend upon arts-related tourism; and total spending by such tourists exceeds £60 million each year. Certain cultural industries to which 1990 is giving substantial impetus are an important source of employment and bring additional export earnings to the regional economy. These include the fashion and design trades, film production and the recording industry.

Investment in Glasgow's infrastructure can be readily justified by direct financial returns. It also gives Glasgow a competitive edge in the search for industrial growth at a time when quality of life is so attenuated in other cities and employers are looking to relocate. Research evidence is there to reassure disbelievers, and substantiate an impressive number of claims about the economic benefits accruing to Glasgow as a result of its year as European Cultural Capital.

1990 and its events are without precedent – one thousand public events; a further one thousand local events; performers and artists from twenty-three countries; thirty major new works commissioned in the performing and visual arts; forty world premières in theatre, dance and music; 125 exhibitions; 1,200 performances and sixty sporting events. Glasgow is presenting an event of considerable scale.

Several of the previous European Cultural Capitals approached the organization of their programmes through a predetermined set of abstract themes. Amsterdam gave focus to ideas, cultural exchange and confrontation. Berlin emphasized the importance of European artistic development and innovation, and drew attention to the city's position in Europe, both East and West. In Paris, the programme coincided with celebrations for the Bicentennial of the French Revolution. Such themes can provide cohesion, but they can also impose restrictions.

Glasgow's 1990 programme sets out to include – rather than restrict or exclude. To show the cultural individuality of the city, every institution and everybody could play a part. Recognizing the importance of crossing borders, contributions from European and non-European countries would be willingly embraced. Ours is a programme in which every kind of event is happily accommodated. This is deliberate.

Still, at the very centre are notions of cultural relevance and quality; of connections to be made and associations to be discovered. Many of the most important events of 1990 explore the special nature of Glasgow. The city's vigorous cultural potential is on display within an international context. This makes for a powerful statement. But 1990 is also a celebration. Entertainment in its broadest sense – and enjoyment for everyone – is essential to the year's success.

Throughout 1990, no one should lose sight of its foundations – the people of Glasgow; the artists and the organizers, the doers and spectators. This vibrant mix of personalities has brought about a measure of inspiration that makes special things happen. Some had ideas and dreams; others offered money and resources. Politicians, business people, educators, individuals from many different places, people of various persuasions, some young, others not so young; all kinds of people who simply wanted to express something, do something, create something about or in their city – it is these people to whom 1990 belongs.

And we do not forget the people who have come to join in, our guests and visitors. People from all over the world who have accepted invitations to return to, or discover for the first time, a city which has earned the respect of Europe. 1990 belongs to them too.

The city is the setting. Glasgow and its surrounding region become a stage. The sedate magnificence of a Victorian past cohabits with the leaner energy of the new; Old Glasgow and New Glasgow side by side. Everyone has his or her own Glasgow; it is a city with many faces; and pride of place is invested in them all. Of course, not all of the rough spots have been smoothed out. Glasgow is a real city after all.

The time has an invigorating ring to it – 1990. A new year. A new decade. It's a year during which, once again, Glasgow renews its hundred year-old tradition of throwing open its doors to the world with a great exhibition. It's also a year in which this city is redefining the proper standing culture deserves in contemporary society and celebrating the validity and worth of the many ways in which it finds expression. And what is particularly heartening is that 1990 is a matter of common ownership. It belongs to Glasgow. And Glasgow belongs to you.

In this book many different writers and artists tell something of the story unfolding during this, the year in which Glasgow rejoices in Europe's most coveted cultural civic honour.

Parts of this remarkable story will be told by simply recounting facts. Some parts need personal description. And still others must be told through poetry, song, or through the languages of pictures and design.

This book provides a collective glimpse of a great city in a very important year. It's the book of the time, the place and, above all, it's the book of the people. That's what 1990 is all about.

Glasgow 1990 would like to thank the following companies, organizations and individuals for generously supporting events and projects that are part of the Cultural Capital of Europe celebrations.

PRIME SPONSORS *Those who have contributed in excess of £100,000*

BP Exploration

Bank of Scotland

Black Bottle Whisky

British Telecom West of Scotland District

British Gas

Matthew Gloag & Son Ltd *Proprietors of The Famous Grouse Scotch Whisky*

Sponsors who have contributed cash, goods or services

Aggreko
Matthew Algie & Company Ltd
Banks Wood & Partners
(*Chartered Quantity Surveyors*)
Brechin Robb
Britannia Life
British Aerospace
British Airways
Cameron House Hotel
Coloroll Edinburgh Crystal
Citicorp/Citibank
Ernst & Young
Glasgow Herald & Evening Times
Goldberg Family Charitable Trust
Guinness plc
IBM in Scotland
Linn Volvo
McCorquodale (Scotland) Ltd
MacFarlane Group (Clansman) plc
MacMillan Video
MacRoberts
Makro
Mercury Communications
Donald Murray Paper
Northern Light
National Westminster Bank
Royal Mail Glasgow Letters District
Radio Scan Ltd
Schroder Investment Management Ltd
Scottish Brewers Limited

Scottish Equitable Life Assurance Society
Scottish Industrial & Trade Exhibitions Ltd
(*A member of the Andry Montgomery Group*)
Scottish Mutual
Shell UK
Stella Artois
Stock Group/Campbell Neill & Co Ltd (Stockbrokers)
Alexander Stone Foundation
3i
TSB Bank Scotland plc
Tarmac Construction
Taylor Woodrow Group
Wm Teacher & Sons Ltd
United Distillers
Isidore & David Walton Foundation
Wylies Ltd
Wylie Shanks Chartered Architects
Yard Limited

Acknowledgements

The events of 1990 are the culmination of a process during which many people and organizations have worked together in partnership.

The Festivals Office of Glasgow District Council would like to acknowledge individually each one of the people who have joined in these partnerships: however the book itself is not big enough to list them.

Particular acknowledgement must go, however, to the Lord Provost, Leader, Councillors and staff of Glasgow District Council for their hard work and support in making sure, first of all that Glasgow received the accolade, and then that 1990 would be a year to remember for all Glaswegians and visitors.

The Convenor, Leader, Councillors and staff of Strathclyde Regional Council have also given their wholehearted support and worked very closely with the District Council throughout the planning process. Through them the European Cultural Capital programme has been spread throughout the Region.

The Greater Glasgow Tourist Board has been central to the event since it was first the gleam of an idea. It has enthused many, and stimulated very productive links with the Scottish Tourist Board and the British Tourist Authority.

The Scottish Development Agency and its staff have also played a significant role in assisting the District Council with 1990, and the Festivals Office is grateful to them.

At UK level the Minister for the Arts steered the accolade through Europe and then backed Glasgow with enthusiasm.

Many sponsors, donors and benefactors from the private sector are acknowledged elsewhere in The Book. There are thousands more working in companies, or working as individuals, who have put heart, soul and imagination into making Glasgow a city which deserves the title Cultural Capital of Europe.

The Book is dedicated to everyone who has helped but especially to the people of Glasgow and their city, without whom it would not have been possible.

All information on events in 1990 contained in The Book is correct at the time of going to press (December 1989) but may be subject to alterations. Please check local press for final details.

With thanks to students: *Allan Martin, Colin Waddell, Rachel, Meehan, Allan Arneil* and acting Head of Department of Illustration and Design at Glasgow School of Art, *Penny Hudd.*

PRIME SPONSORS *Those who have contributed in excess of £100,000*

Lilley Group

Scottish Amicable Life Assurance Society

Tennents

The Royal Bank of Scotland

Whyte & Mackay Distillers

Donors

Angus Modelmakers Ltd
BDO Binder Hamlyn
Bank of England
George Boyd & Co
W Grant Cochrane Esq
Covell Matthews Architects
Peter Dominic Ltd
P R Duff & Son
Elite Bedding & Furniture Group
Gibson & Goold
Louise Grace Electrical Ltd
Sir William Halcrow & Partners
Gordon Harris & Partners
Hill Samuel Bank
JMP Consultants
Jacobs & Turner Ltd (Trespass)
Knight Wendling Ltd
Murray & Muir Chartered Surveyors
Office International
E C Riach Chartered Architects
Robins McTear Ltd
Ryden Property Consultants &
Chartered Surveyors
Sime Malloch Ltd
Gary Sinclair (Scotland) Ltd
R J Steiner Esq
Stockwell China Bazaar
Mr & Mrs G Sutherland
Thomas & Adamson
Transport & General Workers Union
Waterman Partners
John Watson & Co Ltd
Wimpey Homes Holdings Ltd

Benefactors

Ailsa Trucks (Northern) Ltd
Breval Technical Services Ltd
Building Design Partnership
Bulten Limited
Doig & Smith
Richard Ellis Chartered Surveyors
Hewden Stuart plc
Holford Associates
The Holmes Partnership
McGrigor Donald
Montagu Evans
Shanks McEwan Group plc
Sheraton Caltrust plc
Standard Life
Turner & Townsend
F L Walker & Company CA
The Weir Group plc
Wiltshier Scotland Ltd

GLASGOW THE BOOK 1990

contents

Cover image
by Fraser Taylor

Inside front
cover poem
by Edwin Morgan

James Jennings

Susan Baird

Charles Gray

Pat Lally

Joseph Davie

Robert Palmer

Kevin Low

Fraser Taylor

Michael Russell

Robert Palmer

Margo MacDonald

Jane Fraser

CONTENTS

CONTENTS

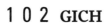

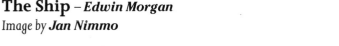

the book

GLASGOW IS FROM AN ORIGINAL IDEA BY ST MUNGO (PLUS OF COURSE, A FISH, A BELL AND A TREE). THE BOOK – GLASGOW 1990 IS FROM ORIGINAL IDEAS BY MORE PEOPLE THAN IT IS POSSIBLE TO LIST. THE PEOPLE OF GLASGOW, IN FACT.

There are many guidebooks to Glasgow itself. This is not one of them. There are many listings of events – daily, weekly, monthly. This is not a listing. The Book is an event – one of the events of what promises to be an action-packed year. It is an event which is designed to go behind the media images of Glasgow 1990, and behind the myriad of other happenings and organized events. The Book is an attempt to distil the flavour of the year into both a forward vision, and a backward glance.

The Book – Glasgow 1990 is a slice of life, a cross-section of a city and a year. For both inhabitants and visitors it should provide a companion and a souvenir.

Each of its contributors – famous, infamous and not famous at all – has something to say about Glasgow in 1990, and each of its artists has a view of the year that is original and challenging.

Whether you are reading this in January 1990 or re-reading it in December 2010 The Book should create enthusiasm, excitement and hope. That's what 1990 will do.

Read The Book and live, remember, and build on the year.
THERE'S A LOT GLASGOWING ON – and there always will be!

Book Mark – Image by **Neil Meechan**
             – Designed by **The Yellow Pencil Company**
Postcards   – Images by **Fraser Taylor, Willie Rodger,**
             Teresa Kerr, Andy Foley
Car Sticker – Photograph by **James Mair**
             – Designed by **The Yellow Pencil Company**

having fun

R O B E R T   P A L M E R

:le by
ert Palmer
atre Director
Playwright,''
'the man in
e 1990''.

Glasgow has at its heart a desire to show OFF! The chain of Glasgow's Great Exhibitions proves it!

The first Glasgow International Exhibition in 1888 celebrated past achievements, and future optimism. Both this event and the exhibition of 1901 demonstrated industrial diversity, innovation, progress in art and education, inventiveness in architecture and an international outlook.

In 1911, Glasgow did it again by staging the Scottish Exhibition of National History, Art and Industry, and Glasgow asserted itself against the background of massive unemployment and poverty with a fourth Exhibition in 1938. The (unknowingly ironic) themes of world peace and friendship mingled with the familiar – progress, industry, art, and architecture.

Glasgow asserted itself against the background of massive unemployment and poverty…

The Glasgow Garden Festival of 1988 was a modern descendent of these earlier events. This Festival gave a boost to the local and regional economy, commerce and tourism by means of inventive land reclamation associated with urban regeneration. The garden theme dominated. This should have been no surprise to a city which has gained world recognition for its parks and green spaces.

Each of these Great Exhibitions has expressed something of the city's indomitable spirit, and has provided much in the way of fun and entertainment. Each has left behind a legacy, sometimes lasting only a little while, and sometimes standing the test of time for enjoyment by future generations. Regrettably, the Doulton Fountain, a lasting memory of 1888 is now in a state of embarrassing disrepair. But Kelvingrove Art Gallery and Museum which began with the profits of the first Great Exhibition was completed by 1901, and remains an important reminder.

…world recognition for its parks and green spaces.

Little remains from 1911, but the Palace of Art from 1938 is used today as a resource centre for Strathclyde Regional Council. The 1988 Garden Festival left 120 acres where attractive housing and leisure developments are to be built. These improvements and the Bell's Bridge, the first pedestrian footbridge built across the Clyde for 130 years, are fitting and enduring memorials. →

**Image by
Jane Frazer**

*. . . standing the test of time
for enjoyment by future
generations.*

And what will be left after 1990? One of the architectural legacies is Glasgow's new International Concert Hall, a £27 million cultural investment, more than just a symbolic gesture to Glasgow's cultural focus. There is the McLellan Galleries completely refurbished for 1990 as a major national venue for exhibitions. Glasgow's former Museum of Transport has been transformed into one of the most exciting performance and exhibition spaces in Europe, renamed Tramway.

There is the development of Scotland Street School, designed by Charles Rennie Mackintosh, into a Museum of Education, and the building of the House for an Art Lover, from original Mackintosh designs.

There is a renovation of twenty-two massive archways underneath Glasgow's Central Railway Station, the stonecleaning of 125 buildings and the floodlighting of eighty of these. Repairs, redevelopment, rehousing and upgrading, changes to the Citizens Theatre, Tron Theatre, the Third Eye Centre, Hunterian Art Gallery, Glasgow Film Theatre, Glasgow Art Gallery and Museum, Burrell Collection and People's Palace, will all remain as reminders of the cultural year.

The evidence of these new physical structures and improvements are visible legacies. So too are new organizations, although it is sometimes difficult to predict which ones will continue into the future. The new festivals of choral, organ, country and western and early music, all of which were initiated through the impetus of 1990, are examples.

Glasgow has now established itself as a major destination for important international artists, performers and sporting events – world orchestras, dance, drama and opera companies, exhibitions and tournaments. These attractions will continue so long as Glasgow maintains an active impresariat with entrepreneurial and creative flair.

There are the significant and varied initiatives which are being undertaken by local activists in areas such as Cranhill, Govan, Castlemilk, the east end, Priesthill, Gorbals, Easterhouse, Garnethill, the south side and so many other places.

Inspiration and leadership have enabled so many hundreds of local groups to do things they otherwise may not have attempted. With increased skills, additional confidence and an expanded network of contacts, the legacy of 1990 will contribute to the quality of our lives.

That legacy will be powerful.

having fun

**Article by
Margo MacDonald**
*Former MP, now
Scots television
journalist.*

MARGO MACDONALD

On a summer Saturday afternoon, is there any greater pleasure to be extracted from Glasgow, Cultural Capital of Europe 1990, than the Keelies' Crawl . . . all the way along Argyle Street from the Saltmarket, round into Buchanan Street and up to Sauchiehall Street?

In Glasgow, the tourists don't get a look in. The seats in the pedestrianized bits of the city centre have been thoughtfully placed so as to facilitate a good view of street performance, as well as provide a convenient place to rest the poly bags before tackling the Savoy Centre, or for him to wait for her, and her sister, to re-emerge from the Argyle Arcade.

There's always been performances on Glasgow's streets, but global warming and leisure-time shopping habits have combined to elbow out the moothie players from draughty doorways and usher in mime artists, pavement artists, jugglers, jazz musicians, break dancers and, it has to be admitted, not a few highland dancers as well.

Streetbiz artists who performed with chalk-white faces and/or classical guitars didn't necessarily go down a bomb just for being there and contributing to the general vitality of the city centre during a festival of street entertainment. Yet every week, some very good →

JANUARY

Keeping Glasgow in Stitches

JAN TO DEC

THE ART GALLERY AND MUSEUM, KELVINGROVE

A year long, city-wide project to capture the spirit of the city in fabric. Working from a base in Kelvingrove, local people will marry their ideas and talents to make twelve large calendar hangings.

This vivid and unique calendar will have a permanent home in Glasgow after 1990. Come and lend a hand, or just watch, as fabric and thread turn into evocative pictures of Glaswegian life.

The project is being co-ordinated by Needleworks, a community sewing enterprise in nearby Partick.

Changing Places

JAN TO DEC

WORLDWIDE

Painters, photographers, sculptors, printmakers, textile designers . . . We welcome artists from East and West Europe and North America, changing places with our own for periods of up to three months. Glasgow-based artists will be working in Moscow, Berlin, Helsinki, Athens, Turin . . . Glasgow School of Art, Glasgow Sculpture Studios, Glasgow Print Studio and WASPS (Working and Artist Studio Provision Scotland) are involved.

The Chinese New Year

JAN TO MAR

THE ART GALLERY AND MUSEUM, KELVINGROVE

For the Chinese, 1990 is the year of the horse. So, at Kelvingrove Art Gallery there's an exhibition about horses: from workhorses to warhorses to racehorses. And it's about people too: our attitudes towards horses and how we've used them.

musicians, popular and classical, can collect sizeable, intent audiences.

I confess that, perversely, it's these talented, dedicated performers who can make me feel uncomfortable with the whole idea of street theatre.

On a dreich day in Glasgow, I feel as guilty as any bloated capitalist should at the beautiful sound, and sorry sight of thin young music students playing in the street. They're not playing for kicks, or for practice; they're playing because they need the money. I confess that I love the music, and I admire their guts. But on a raw Saturday morning in Sauchiehall Street, I can take no pleasure from their presence.

. . . I love the music, and I admire their guts.

The source of my discomfort is, of course, the feeling that, however much I drop in the violin case or the battered box, it won't be enough to buy off the indignity they might feel. Seasoned theatrical performers have told me that they've felt cheap when they've played the streets. I know the feeling, having given it laldy on countless street corners myself. And yet, it can be a great feeling, too; the feeling that you're in the right place, at the right time, doing the right things to interest, amuse or intrigue your fellow citizens.

I think the difference lies in the motivation, material and atmosphere. Sunshine and warmth help, and if the material of the performance is relevant, whether it be musical, dramatic or political, an audience can be collected and a rapport struck. But most important of all, the performer must want to perform.

1990 should provide the setting and atmosphere for a great extension of street theatre in Glasgow. Performers from all over will converge on the city, and Glaswegians and tourists alike will expect the streets to provide a rich mix of entertainment and interest.

So while I don't really expect to be assailed by Pavarotti while I'm diving in and out the shops during the summer sales, I hope I'll have the pleasure of settling down for the odd ten minutes in Buchanan Street for a bit of contemporary drama, or restoration comedy performed by actors in the professional theatre groups who'll visit the city's halls and theatres throughout the year of culture. That way, everybody in Glasgow will be able to get in on the act.

BLACK BOTTLE

A WEE BIT OUT OF THE ORDINARY

JANUARY

Dangerous to Know

8 TO 25 JAN
GLASGOW FILM THEATRE

A varied selection from the London Lesbian and Gay Film Festival. New and rare films from around the world examine the history and current attitudes to homosexuality. Discussions and seminars will expand upon topics raised in such features as the 1986 Hong Kong production, Peking Opera Blues and Desire, which traces the situation of the German gay community in Germany up to the Second World War.

Scottish International Piano Competition

9 TO 14 JAN
ROYAL SCOTTISH ACADEMY OF MUSIC & DRAMA/ GLASGOW CITY HALL

The Competition involves approximately thirty competitors, each initially performing a twenty-five minute recital of work by Bach, Chopin, Liszt, Haydn and Mozart. It builds to a climax with the three finalists playing with the Scottish National Orchestra directed by Bryden Thomson. This will be relayed live from the City Hall by BBC Scotland Television.

Degas' Images of Women

15 JAN TO 25 FEB
THE BURRELL COLLECTION

In more than two thirds of Degas works — paintings, pastels, etchings and sculptures — women are the subject.
Degas scholar, Richard Kendall has selected three themes for the show exploring this aspect of the artist's work: Women of Leisure, Working Women and Women in Private.

a laugh – with Tom Conti

CHRIS DOLAN

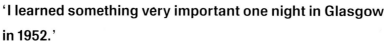

Image by
Willie Rodger

*Glasgow
is Garrulous
Lively
Adaptable
Sharp
Generous
Optimistic.*

Article by
Tom Conti

*Scots actor of
international
renown.*

**'I learned something very important one night in Glasgow
in 1952.'**

Tom Conti was sitting in his living room surrounded by guitars and
records, sheet music spilling from the old grand piano. He was resting – in
the literal sense. His last film *Shirley Valentine* had just become the top
box-office success in Britain. Conti was not only at home, but at home
with himself, relishing the opportunity to talk about subjects close to his
heart: Music, Wit and Glasgow.

'It was while I was watching Gigli – the greatest tenor alive! I knew there
was something special about this man, but it wasn't until I began acting
that I understood what it was: Generosity – simple, colossal Generosity.
Gigli genuinely wanted to sing for the audience. There was a real love
between the man and the people of Glasgow that night. And boy, did Gigli
sing! Encore after encore, the audience wild with joy. When he appeared
on stage for the last time, he had his hat and coat on, ready to run for the
last train! Now there's a lesson for a young performer to learn.'

Conti throws his head back and laughs joyfully at the memory. Praising
the work of the Scottish Baroque Ensemble, he gets up to find a particular
record from his vast collection, but is diverted by the subject of Pavarotti's
1990 concert in Glasgow:

'Pavarotti is the reigning master in a golden lineage: Caruso, Gigli,
Bjorling. To hear Pavarotti now at the height of his talent will be
sensational. Glasgow will love him. He'll love Glasgow.

'There is a sense of harsh reality at the heart of Glaswegian humour. There
was a play I did years ago, called *Whose Life Is It Anyway?* about a man
who was paralysed and wanted to die. In the script he was from England
somewhere, but I changed him into a Scot, because it allowed the humour
to be harsher. His anger had a real comic bitterness to it.'

On the subject of brutal humour, Conti remembers having to fight hard to
retain the final scene of *Reuben Reuben* – the film he received an Oscar
nomination for. Gowan McGland, the hero, is making a half-hearted
attempt at hanging himself, when suddenly his dog rushes to the chair he
is standing on, knocks it over, and does the job for him.

' "You can't do that to the hero" we were told. But I knew it would work.
Being hung by a dug! Glasgow audiences would appreciate that!' →

'At funerals, four
rounds of whisky
were considered
due to wounded
affection and
departed worth,
and respect was
shown to the dead
by the intoxication
of the living.'
(Social Life in
Scotland – Rev
Charles Rogers,
The Grampian
Club, 1884)

'I was in a posh little coffee shop a few weeks ago in Central Station, and this wee bloke comes in, with his bunnet all sidey-ways, a bit unsteady on his toes and slurring his words. He shouts out:

"Ten-shun! Royal Air Force. 1939 to 1945. Squadron B. Fought for ma country…" He takes off his cap and collects money round the tables, and we all gave because there was something very endearing about the guy. When he gets back to the door, he counts his money, stops and says: "Yous are all daft! Ah was never in the bloody Air Force in ma life!" The place erupted. Classic Glasgow humour; those who put in the most money laughed the loudest. I'm not sure you would have got the same reaction in another city.'

Tom Conti treated me to a one-to-one show. We had been talking about Glasgow again, when he remembered a story about a drunk man. Rather than just tell it, Conti got up and acted it.

He had been with some friends at a bus stop in Clyde Street, and they were laughing at a man who was trying to negotiate a half bottle of whisky into his back pocket. Standing in front of me, Conti wavered and swayed around precariously. His feet never moved, but his body tilted over at dangerous angles. I felt myself getting ready to jump out of the way in case he fell on me. His eyes became glazed over, he knit his brow, as he tried to get the imaginary bottle into his pocket.

'We were all laughing at this sight. And then, catastrophe! The bottle fell. Smashed. The laughter cut like that. We were stunned. The poor man stood for a long time, just looking at the bottle, its contents flowing away. You could feel his disbelief at the tragedy that had just happened.

'I wanted that scene in *Reuben Reuben* but we lost it because of time limits. Pity, really.

'When I was wee, shipbuilding was still an energetic industry in Glasgow. It was a rough and frightening place, but exciting. Then, when I went back in the 1970s, I was shocked. The place had really suffered. I was appalled just at the expressions on peoples' faces – looks of despair.

'But Glasgow has got living soul. It's on the way back, and the ability to pull itself up by the bootstraps is the best indication there is of the spirit of the place.

'I would love to make films in Scotland. In fact I'm working right now on a film I want to direct. Scotland is just indescribably beautiful – perfect for film making. The only problem is the weather. Not that it rains all the time – it doesn't. That's the difficulty. You'll be shooting a scene in the rain, when suddenly the sun comes out and shines gloriously!

'The film I have in mind is based on the life of a Scottish folk hero. If we can find the money locally, then we won't have to get involved with American distributors who have a habit of interfering with your screenplay. It's such an ideal place to film, Scotland. There's so much talent around: writers, actors, technicians. The lot. They are all there.'

…he had his hat and coat on, ready to run for the last train! Now there's a lesson…

a laugh – with Jack Webster

JACK WEBSTER

Article by Jack Webster

Columnist on the Glasgow Herald.

Exempting themselves from the reticence generally attributed to the Scots, Glaswegians have never been backward at putting themselves forward. The rest of Britain, and maybe the world, has had to sit up and listen again to the boast that Glasgow's Miles Better. Visitors came flocking to the Garden Festival of 1988 and are doing so again in 1990. But the title of Cultural Capital of Europe is liable, in itself, to stir local humour. No fur-coated fantasies will be allowed to survive if the knickers are not in place.

For all the pretension to better things, Glaswegians like to retain a good footing in their working-class background.

The fashionable status of the city in the eighties has enabled the culture and humour of Glasgow to be exported with unaccustomed ease. The BBC in London, for example, handed over its network output of plays to be produced from the city. People like Billy Connolly had already taken Clydeside humour as far as Drury Lane, popularizing a seam of lavatorial vulgarity which proved to be no flash in the pan!

A new generation of funny people symbolized by none better than Gregor Fisher, is taking Glasgow humour to the wider audience of television through shows like *Naked Video*, matching the network success established by Robbie Coltrane and company in John Byrne's television series of *Tutti Frutti*. (Coltrane's comic genius is being further deployed during the year of culture in comedy at the King's Theatre).

There may be modifications of dialect to suit an alien ear but the foundations of it all go back to that bronchial tenement, which was the real-life home of some of the greatest comics Glasgow and Scotland have ever produced. I am thinking particularly of people like Tommy Morgan, Clairty-Clairty himself, who knew at first hand the poverty of a Bridgeton upbringing and whose audience was in the palm of his hand from the very first mention of the wally-close or the jawbox.

He came from an abundant breed of men who were born to make the whole world laugh. Figures of genius such as Tommy Lorne and Dave Willis, the butcher's boy from Cowcaddens, who modelled himself on the appearance of Charlie Chaplin and could be every bit as funny. If I were asked to nominate the two funniest people I have ever seen on stage, they would both come from Glasgow. One would certainly be Willis.

My other nominee would be the newsagent's son from Riddrie, Rikki Fulton, whose versatility puts him in the top bracket of all-time Scots humorists. It is all the more shameful that the powers-that-be of television in the south have continued to shun his annual *Scotch and Wry* on the network, for fear that those Hogmanay classics might be unintelligible to English ears.

Of course there have been other figures of genius, from Stanley Baxter to Lex McLean. On the writing side, no one has observed the Glasgow scene and expressed it with greater effect than Cliff Hanley, whose *Dancing in the Streets* is surely a classic of its kind.

In the year of culture, Glasgow is being exposed to humour from many an airt. A Comic's Convention will reveal that Desperate Dan and the Broons now compete for public attention with characters who revel in such unthinkable names as Johnny Fartpants. The world allegedly moves on, in all its raw diversity!

The poverty may have gone but mankind manages to replace it with one human dilemma after another. Cynicism abounds in a cold, harsh world where most of us could do with a good old belly-laugh. In the final analysis, I would put my money on Glasgow providing it!

A new generation of funny people…

…the foundations of it all go back to that bronchial tenement…

…men who were born to make the whole world laugh…

JANUARY

Reorienting: Looking East

20 JAN TO 4 MAR
THIRD EYE CENTRE

Glasgow's principal contemporary art space opens its programme for the year with a highly stimulating international group exhibition which examines the synthesis of Eastern and Western culture. The show, curated by leading critic Lynne Cooke, includes works from France and the USA and from four Japanese artists who have never before shown in Britain.

The British Art Show 1990

24 JAN TO 11 MAR
McLELLAN GALLERIES

This month sees the re-opening of the McLellan Galleries in Sauchiehall Street. A £3.5 million refurbishment makes this impressive nineteenth-century building a fitting venue for internationally important visual arts exhibitions and events. Inaugurating its programme for 1990, the McLellan Galleries launches the **British Art Show 1990**, → one of the largest exhibitions of contemporary art ever to tour Britain. This show is about what's new in the visual arts. Recent works by some forty selected British artists will display what's most innovative in painting, sculpture, film, video, installations and performance.

Communicado – Jock Tamson's Bairns

25 JAN TO 24 FEB
THE TRAMWAY

Communicado is the most consistently innovative theatre company in Scotland.

The company has been invited by the City of Glasgow to create the opening production →

Image by
John Rankin
*Photographer
Paisley.*

i belong to Glasgow

J I M M Y   R E I D

Article by
Jimmy Reid
*Journalist and
broadcaster
now columnist
on The Sun.*

To the Glaswegian, art, like beauty, is in the eye of the beholder. A brilliantly structured touchdown can be a work of art to a rugby fan.

A good-looking girl can be a picture. She can also be a picture of health. A good mover is poetry in motion. Anyone who can do something really well, particularly with a touch of elegance, is considered an artist. Excellence and distinction are a kind of beauty, which is art, and therefore part of our culture.

By this reckoning Jim Baxter, of Rangers and Scotland, who played football with nonchalant ease and skill was an artist. He played keepie uppie with the ball at Wembley in a famous Scottish victory, and immediately secured for himself an honoured place in that temple of the mind which is dedicated to Glasgow's cultural heritage.

I knew a burner, an expert with an acetylene torch, who could burn out a circular hole on the shell of a ship with such finesse that there was little left to file down to reach the precise diameter. An awesome skill which made the job of the engineer much easier. To me he was an artist.

When an apprentice engineer in sunny Govan, a riverside community of great character, where a cat with a tail was either a novelty or a tourist, I knew an old fellow, a universal grinder in the toolroom who was looked upon by everyone as an artist. He could machine by eye and only stop to measure with a micrometer when within a few thousands of an inch of the required size. His work was magic.

He was also a drunk. Living permanently in an alcoholic fog. Semi-intoxicated during working hours, he topped up during the evening and became, what is known in these parts, as absolutely blootered. The gaffer reckoned that if he was so brilliant when bevvied up, there was no telling what he was capable of when sober, which was unexpectedly true.

Counsellors brought in by the personnel manager eventually persuaded him to give up demon drink. But his genius departed along with the booze and the gaffer spent a lot of time and his own money trying to get him back on the hooch. →

'During the Reformation the ministers of Glasgow persuaded the magistrates to pull down the Cathedral and build two or three churches from the materials. Workmen were ready to demolish it when the tradesmen of Glasgow threatened to bury them under the rubble if they did. The matter was referred to the King and council who decided in the tradesmen's favour.' **(The History of Glasgow – John McUre, 1830)**

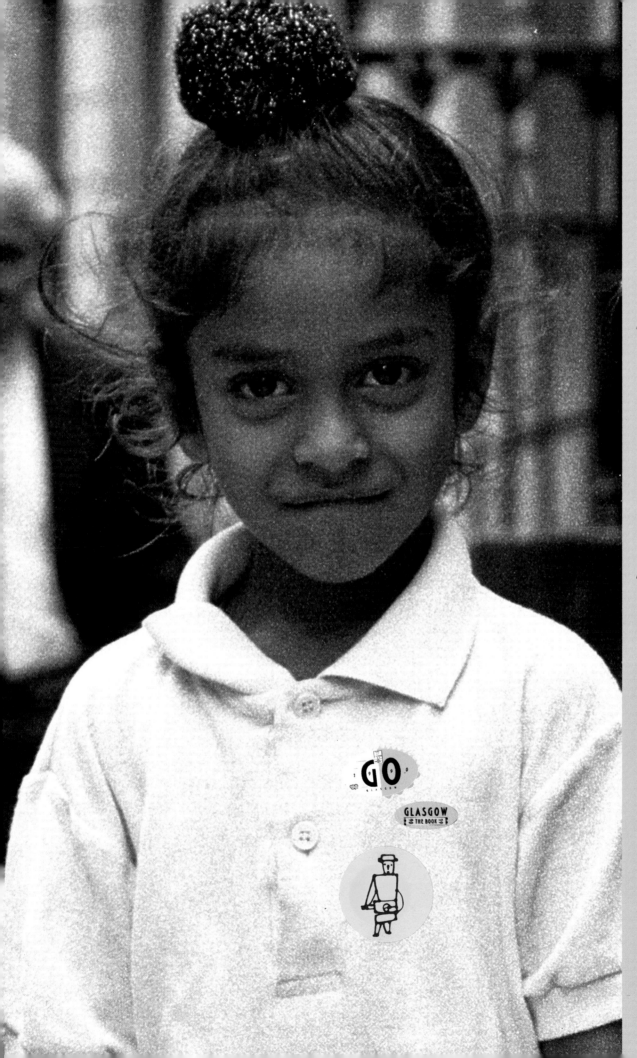

JANUARY

for the Tramway 1990 programme. **Jock Tamson's Bairns** is an operatic theatre piece, a contemporary chronicle of the Scots seen through the eyes of the bairns. The company will use all of the vast public spaces at Tramway making this production one of the most ambitious site-specific performance projects yet mounted there.

Burns Supper

26 JAN
HOSPITALITY INN

A traditional celebration of Scotland's national bard. Shadow Chancellor John Smith will propose the Immortal Memory. And the music will be performed by children from Strathclyde schools. This is a charity night hosted by Strathclyde Regional Council. The proceeds will help Jean Armour Burns Houses and the European Special Olympics in July.

The Chinese New Year

29 JAN
CITY HALL

Chinese New Year actually arrives on 27 January. Two days later a celebration organized by Glasgow's Chinese Community takes place in the City Hall. The programme highlights traditional dancing, folk music and rituals performed by children – who will later be given Chinese lucky money. There's also a music drama. And did someone say something about food?

Dressing The City

JAN TO DEC
CITY CENTRE

Dressing the City is a multifaceted year long project designed to enrich the look of Glasgow during 1990. Artists will be working with various community groups to decorate the city in every way they can. Billboards, buildings and double-decker buses will take on new and surprising appearances.

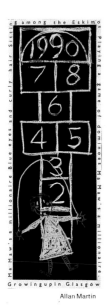

Allan Martin

...fine arts will more or less die, like uprooted plants.

Glasgow's concept of culture is akin to that of the anthropologist. The totality of life in a civilization or community is its culture, including the economy, commerce, jurisprudence, religion, philosophy, morals, science and industry, as well as it's music, literature, theatre and visual arts.

Siphon off the fine arts from the social reality which gave it life, and the fine arts will more or less die, like uprooted plants.

Glasgow, though, never tries to intellectualize its concept of culture, or anything else, for it is profoundly suspicious of intellectuals, except those who have purged themselves of all the pretensions so prone to that ilk. This is why you will find members of Glasgow's intelligentsia imploring, 'Please, believe me, I'm just a punter with a weird job.'

It also partially explains why Stalinist agit-prop art flourishes in corners of Glasgow while it's being dumped in the Soviet Union. It is painters wanting to be more proletarian than the proletariat; portraying workers with granite faces and hands like hams, or as despairing subhumans in the grip of poverty-induced dementia. The only people who enthuse about their work are media art critics from the south-east of England.

Glasgow's workers look and turn away or don't look. This response isn't philistinism but the reaction of people who can tell the difference between art and artifice, the artist and the artful.

...people who can tell the difference between art and artifice, the artist and the artful.

A barmaid who dispensed non-contrived absolutely natural charm along with whisky in a hostelry in the city's Anderston district, which a modern sociologist almost certainly would describe as an area of multiple deprivation, told me of her holiday tour of Italy. She was describing the magnificence of Michelangelo's sculpture of David. 'So beautiful it made me proud to be human.' Maybe, somewhere, at sometime, a learned scholar or noted art critic has paid a better tribute to the genius of a great artist, than this Glasgow housewife, but I doubt it.

Pub debates are to Glasgow what the forum was in Roman times. Debates rage on all sorts of subjects like the sexual proclivities of William Shakespeare and whether these found expression in his sonnets, or about the likelihood of Glasgow Rangers signing a Scot. I have heard a voice from across a crowded bar seeking information. 'Hey Jimmy, who was that b------ who wrote Handel's Largo?'

Debate can often overflow onto the streets at closing time. I once saw a punter outside a pub, holding another by the lapels and stoating his heid aff the wa' (which means repeatedly and rhythmically bouncing his head on the side of a building) while intoning, 'I'm telling you there are forty-nine islands in the Japanese archipelagos.'

...stoating his heid aff the wa'...

I remember coming from a concert by the Scottish National Orchestra in the City Halls to a nearby pub for a little libation and wee chaff about the music and anything else which came to mind. We were joined by a violinist from the orchestra who like me has a marvellous talent for backing horses on their off day. He also played fiddle in a folk band. Some guys in the bar were playing Scottish traditional melodies on a variety of instruments including the penny whistle. One of them who knew my fondness for jazz joined our group to play for me a medley of Duke Ellington numbers, on the harmonica.

We talked about all kinds of music, and horse-racing and the unacceptable power of the big bookmakers and politics, philosophy, nationalism and internationalism and aesthetics, although without mentioning or even thinking of some of these off-putting grandiose titles.

Punters will willingly talk about aesthetics, and have plenty to say on the subject, but not if you use that word. There are those who will only talk if you use that word, and yet have really nothing to say, which won't however, stop them blabbering.

PROUD TO BE PART OF GLASGOW 1990
CULTURAL CAPITAL OF EUROPE.

"La Forza del Destino" by Verdi is the first of Scottish ·ra's special 1990 productions, and it's sponsored by · of Scotland. "The Green City" is to be performed by the Youth and Junior Chorus of the SNO, and sponsored by Bank of Scotland.

Bank of Scotland is also sponsoring the Last Night of the SNO Proms and is a major sponsor of Glasgow Jazz Festival and Mayfest, to mention but a few – and recognising that culture extends beyond the arts, Bank of Scotland is sponsoring, in addition, a number of sports and community events.

In fact, Bank of Scotland is a PRIME SPONSOR – it's official.

it's a small world

Article by

Shereen Nanjiani

A news presenter for STV since 1988.

S H E R E E N   N A N J I A N I

I was driving from Renfrew to Glasgow, the distance was lost in a sunny haze and it seemed as if a great highway opened out across the world. China, Newfoundland, Borneo, India, the green ranches of South America, the golden grain-lands of Canada — all these lay just down there and the giant forests of these shipyards were nothing more than an ant-like industry of man… spider like monsters; H.G. Wells' fantastic creatures from Mars. **(The book of the Clyde – Donald Maxwell, 1927)**

Glasgow has freshened its face. Today it is a place of parks, museums, art galleries, café bars, inner city dwellings, and all-pervading chic. But no one would pretend to have captured, in their brochures and slogans, the heart and soul of a city full of contradictions and contrasts.

Glaswegians were the first to laugh when Glasgow was named Cultural Capital of Europe. To some people in the city, culture is something which develops on damp bedroom walls, and the housing department knows we have plenty of that.

The irony was not lost, either, on those incarcerated in multi-storey flats when Glasgow hosted the 1988 Garden Festival. One person's wide open space, it seemed, was another's window box in a city whose planners had never quite decided what was more desirable.

But the city embraced the Garden Festival wholeheartedly and helped make it the most successful ever staged. From a selfish angle, they had one special reason for doing so. Glaswegians, after all, love a party, even if, strictly speaking, they're not invited.

Neil Kinnock, in the *Glasgow's Miles Better* book shows a real appreciation of what's at the heart of the Glasgow character.

'It isn't that it's got advantages, and it isn't because it's self-satisfied – it's just that people in Glasgow would rather have a laugh than do anything… and a city is, after all, its people much more than its buildings or beauties.'

That's not to say that its people are not interested in its buildings and beauties, but pride in appearance is only one area of interest in a city where, despite all the social and economic problems over the years, people have always taken their pleasures seriously.

None more seriously than football, an obsession which is probably the most accurate barometer of the ups and downs of Glasgow life. Its two major clubs have, on occasions, acted as outstanding ambassadors for the city, but their sectarian rivalry has also given rise to a sense of unease and guilt.

Celtic was founded by Irish priests who had come to work for the poor people of the east end; Rangers has its roots embedded in a solid tradition of refusing to sign Catholics. The result is an ugly scar on Glasgow's face. →

Image by

Ingborg Smith

'Glasgow not too big, not too small. More bottle banks please.'

FEBRUARY

New Moves

1 JAN TO MAR
THIRD EYE CENTRE

The Third Eye Centre's annual **New Moves** season has quickly established itself as the Scottish platform for the newest work in experimental dance and movement from Britain and abroad. **New Moves** will take place during concentrated periods between January and March. Alongside public performances, the programme includes workshops and teaching. **New Moves** features several guest artists and companies, and ends with performances by leading foreign groups at the Royal Scottish Academy of Music and Drama.

February Music

3 FEB
CITY HALL/ROYAL SCOTTISH ACADEMY OF MUSIC & DRAMA

During February, the Scottish National Orchestra and the Scottish Chamber Orchestra are staging nine concerts. These will highlight works by Prokofiev, Borodin, Mussorgsky, Rachmaninov and Tchaikovsky. The SNO also plays Martinu's First Symphony (3 Feb) as part of a season marking the composer's centenary. At the Royal Scottish Academy of Music and Drama, there is a celebrity concert with cellists Paul and Maud Tortelier. Philip Ledger conducts the Academy Orchestra (8 Feb). The programme includes the Vivaldi Double Concerto and Paul Tortelier's own Concerto for Two Instruments.

Trials of Strength

10 TO 11 FEB
KELVIN HALL

Almost 100 years ago, the first recorded indoor tug-of-war championships took place in Glasgow between the Glasgow and Dublin police departments.

…culture is something which develops on damp bedroom walls.

…people have always taken their pleasures seriously.

…tolerate its own cultural gulfs the way it has those of others.

But just when bigotry was becoming an embarrassing backdrop to the city's new enlightenment, traditional values were turned upside-down. Rangers signed a Catholic. And Maurice Johnston was not only a Catholic, but also a former Celtic player who had been about to re-join his old club in the east end.

But there are many more obstacles still to be overcome, and the very fact that we still have separate schools for Catholic and non-Catholic means, that in the short-term at least, religious division remains an accepted part of life.

Ironically, it was this structure for providing the Catholic Church with what they wanted, which made the implementation of Rangers' sectarian policy a relatively simple task: 'What school did you go to, son?' had been a standard interview question for Rangers talent scouts.

But we go on striking a balance between so many conflicting cultures, which other cities have found impossible to achieve! At one school, for example, as many as nineteen languages are spoken, each, of course, with its own particular Glaswegian nuances!

This open tolerance of other races could be explained by Glasgow's own peculiar race issue. That it has not suffered the racial violence experienced in similar cities is, perhaps, due to the fact that Glaswegians have been less concerned with colour and more with which side of the sectarian debate the individual places himself. Only in Glasgow could there be a Catholic school with more Muslim pupils than Catholic.

After everything that has been accomplished it should not be too much to hope that the Glasgow of the nineties could learn to tolerate its own cultural gulfs the way it has those of others.

Some may say this is more a fantasy than a real possibility, but then many things have happened in this city which the sceptics said could never happen.

After all, who would have predicted that a Glaswegian with a name like Shereen Nanjiani would one day be reading the news on Scottish Television?

it's a small world

Article by
Joe Farrell
Lectures in Italian at the University of Strathclyde.

Scots went to Italy in search of ideas and artistic inspiration…

JOE FARRELL

In any consideration of the forces which have shaped modern Glasgow, it would be easy, but unforgivable, to forget the Italian element.

If identifying the Glasgow Italians in a telephone directory is a simple enterprise, locating the community itself, and assessing its impact, is more complex. Integration has been complete. All that remains of the immigration which brought families from the villages of Picinisco and Barga are a random selection of thoroughly Scots lawyers, accountants and teachers – and those who have remained faithful to the original occupations as café owners and fish and chip merchants.

There might be something misplaced in any search for traces in buildings or in stone to the Glasgow Italians. Monuments are the work of the powerful and, whatever they subsequently became, the Italians did not arrive in Scotland

prosperous or financially dominant. They were poor folk who, like immigrants the world over, found earning a living at home difficult and went elsewhere in the hope of bettering themselves. The aim was to survive, possibly in comfort, but the unprivileged have to aim to integrate and accept.

The most visible and lasting monuments associated with Italy in the city have nothing to do with the Italo-Scots. Down the centuries, Scots went to Italy in search of ideas and artistic inspiration because well before there was a Common Market to award the title, Italy was the undisputed cultural centre of Europe.

Glaswegians who made that journey did return enriched, and in their turn they enriched their native city. For whatever reason – and it may be due to the influence of John Ruskin on the Victorian imagination – the distinctive style →

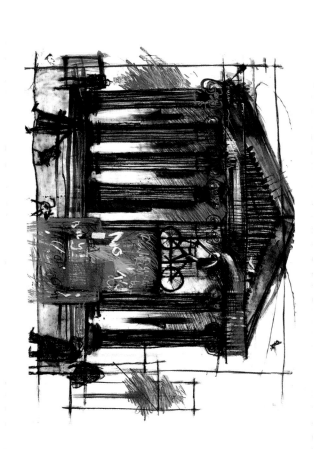

GLASGOW 1990

CULTURAL CAPITAL OF EUROPE

Theresa

GLASGOW 1990

CULTURAL CAPITAL OF EUROPE

Michael Taylor

GLASGOW 1990

CULTURAL CAPITAL OF EUROPE

Fraser Taylor

GLASGOW 1990

CULTURAL CAPITAL OF EUROPE

Andrew Foley

of Venetian architecture seems to have held a special appeal for Glasgow architects. The Ca d'Oro in Gordon Street was inspired by the beautiful Renaissance palace of the same extravagant name – the House of Gold – which stands overlooking the Grand Canal in Venice, and when the Glasgow version was destroyed by fire in the early 1980s, public opinion demanded that it be reconstructed as it was, where it was.

It would be curious to know what the Italians themselves thought of these transplants when they began to arrive in Glasgow from the 1880s onwards. Various attempts, none entirely satisfactory, have been made to explain why they came to Scotland in the first place, and certainly some only settled here because they were unable to go to the more common destinations of the migrants. The Fazzis, now in their third generation, run an excellent shop of Italian produce which has always been indispensable both to the Italian community and to Glaswegian gourmets, but the founders of the family firm only made Glasgow their home because, having got as far as the temporary immigration centre on the Statue of Liberty island, they were refused permission to proceed any further in the USA.

... settled here because they were unable to go to the more common destinations.

No one bothered to keep accurate statistics, but there are undoubtedly thousands of contemporary Glaswegians who can trace their origins back to Barga. They were uniformly an independent-minded lot, and very few of the incomers had any intentions of working for any other employer. Their ambition was to be their own master. Their employment in the early days was varied but the bulk drifted towards what is grandly known as the 'catering sector'.

The modest café was commonplace in Italy but an innovation to Scotland for which the Italians were largely responsible. In its own small way, its introduction was a revolutionary departure, and one which added colour to the life of the nation, since it provided working-class men and, more especially, women with a social meeting place. Some people regarded this novelty with dread and suspicion, and, Scotland being what

it is, there were those who were convinced that the café could only bode ill for the moral welfare of the people.

there were those who were convinced that the café could only bode ill for the moral welfare of the people.

This desire to remain independent, allied with the choice of employment, meant that there never was any Little Italy in Glasgow. The Jews from Eastern Europe, like later immigrants from the Indian sub-continent, settled initially in the Gorbals, but the Italians spread out. No matter how prosperous, each district of the city could support only one or two catering establishments, and the Italo-Scots moved to where the work was to be found. They were thus from the very outset compelled to immerse themselves in the host culture. If this process favoured integration, it made the preservation of a distinctive culture difficult. The children born to the immigrants in Glasgow rarely acquired the command of their own language which would have come from mixing in an extended community with a similar background, and settled for being Italo-Scots and subsequently for being Scots with Italian names.

FEBRUARY

Now, the world's top three tug-of-war nations are the Republic of Ireland, England and Switzerland. And they'll be sending teams to Glasgow. So will France, Germany, Holland, Italy, Sweden and Spain, all taking part in the open competition at the first ever indoor UK Tug-of-War Championships. The UK championship itself will be contested by the four home nations and teams representing Jersey and Guernsey.

Coltrane at the King's

13 TO 17 FEB
KING'S THEATRE

The King's Theatre, one of Scotland's best-loved theatres for pantomime, popular theatre, entertainment and light opera will play a full part in the 1990 celebrations.

Following the 1989 pantomime, Borderline Theatre Company presents the English language première of Dario Fo's famous comedy **Mistero Buffo (The Comic Mysteries)**. Drawing on the counter-culture of the Middle Ages, apocryphal tales, ghost stories, legends and jokes, Fo's masterpiece is a hilarious history of Christendom. It'll star Robbie Coltrane, and nobody could perform these tall and irreverent tales better. Coltrane's reputation, now international, is based on superb stage craft – especially his talents for mimicry and characterization, and pure comic skill.

A great first for Coltrane and Borderline, and a superb beginning to the King's 1990. Not to be missed.

New Lang Syne

17 FEB
THE ART GALLERY AND MUSEUM, KELVINGROVE

Many hundreds of people – with or without singing experience – are gathering to sing a →

Image by
Annabel Wright
Illustrator based in Glasgow. Enjoys going to the speedway.

a night out — 'there's no business like it!'

JOHN MILLAR

Article by
John Millar
Television Editor of the Daily Record. Supports Hearts!

On the night of Saturday 17 August 1849 there was a comedy being performed at the Theatre Royal. During the show a small fire was spotted and extinguished by a man working there. However, the fire alarm and the sight of a fireman scared the audience and caused them to run in fright for the exits. Five hundred people from the gallery ran down the stairwell in fear, causing a huge crush and resulting in the deaths of sixty-five people. **(John Urie, 1908)**

Long before Hollywood movie-maker George Lucas had breathed life into Han Solo and Luke Skywalker, Glasgow folk knew that the Empire strikes back.

The Empire, which was every bit as chilling as the menacing Darth Vader, was the city's most notorious theatre.

It was on its boards that showbiz legends were born and reputations left in tatters. If the audience at The Empire didn't like a performance, the star didn't suffer something as ordinary as boos and bad reviews; he left scarred for life.

The classic example is still recalled today by Empire victim Des O'Connor. His first professional booking, and almost his last, was in front of 3,000 Glaswegians, who, rather like Queen Victoria, were not amused by his act.

As he faced row after row of hostile, unsmiling faces, Des decided that a man had to do what a man had to do … so he pretended to faint.

An extreme way of escaping from that dread stage, perhaps. But other stars, who soldiered on, despite getting the 'treatment' from an Empire audience, probably wished they'd thought of Des's dodge.

It would have been one way of avoiding the humiliating heckling that greeted a certain comedy double act. One half of the duo had gone on stage first. When his partner joined him on stage, a voice from the darkness moaned loudly, 'Oh no, there's two of them!'

But today the city's audiences are famed for the warmth of their greeting and their appreciation. Doubters should simply be reminded that there was much gnashing of teeth from rock stars such as Rod Stewart, The Who and Status Quo – to name but a few – when it was announced that the Apollo – a theatre regarded by many as Britain's premier rock venue – was to be demolished.

The stars knew that they were guaranteed a night of rapturous applause whenever they played the Apollo. On many nights the audience got so carried away that the theatre's circle actually bounced up and down! →

… the audience got so carried away that the theatre's circle actually bounced up and down!

… showbiz legends were born and reputations left in tatters.

FEBRUARY

varied and fun programme of popular favourites. This is the first event of 1990 for the Singing Audience who had such success in the past few months and who were such a hit at Hogmanay in George Square. Call That Singing! want more and more people to join in, have fun and sing in a variety of events. During 1990 – *everybody* will participate – *everybody* will be a performer.

The Mikado

20 TO 24 FEB
KING'S THEATRE

The Savoy Club, one of Glasgow's amateur theatrical companies, this month celebrates its golden jubilee with a new production of the classic Gilbert and Sullivan operetta **The Mikado**. The other companies, among whom are the Lyric, Glasgow Grand, the Apollo Players and of course The Gang Show, promise that this year's contributions will be something equally special.

John Logie Baird

24 FEB TO 24 MAR
COLLINS GALLERY

The centenary of John Logie Baird's birth in 1988 re-kindled interest in his pioneering work. His prodigious research in the fields of television, radar and fibre optics have had a profound influence on contemporary life. This exhibition recalls the significance of his inventions and discoveries and celebrates his achievements.

The exhibition is the beginning of a series of projects on John Logie Baird initiated by Strathclyde University – where Baird himself studied.

They live life as though it was a movie, and their wit is rapid-fire.

That brilliance shines as strongly as ever... thanks to the abundance of fresh talent which continues to spring from the city.

While the rockers of Glasgow may be more overt in displaying their feelings, audiences throughout the showbiz spectrum are no less involved. Remember, we are talking about a city where the breadth of entertainment on offer more than matches anything in the country. Where else but Glasgow, could you have Sydney Devine giving his unique rendition of numbers like 'Ti-nee Bub-bells' at one venue at the same time as an awe-inspiring piece of epic theatre such as *The Mahabharata* is being staged elsewhere. Contrasts of that sort will abound during 1990: from the Bolshoi Opera to the Special Olympics; from the Henry Moore Exhibition to the Country Music Festival; and from the Eight Hundredth Glasgow Fair to Pavarotti.

The city thrives on showbiz, and the reason why is obvious. Glasgow's citizens are larger than life. They live life as though it was a movie, and their wit is rapid-fire. 1990 will be yet another stage for the live Glaswegian performance that happens every year.

Given all this it isn't surprising that Glasgow's tradition of producing stars should continue to prosper. The list of the showbiz stars, who can have as their anthem 'I Belong To Glasgow' is impressive indeed.

To mention them all would mean taking over most of this book, so I'll settle for listing a few of my favourites, all landmarks in the city's showbiz history.

The legendary comic Lex McLean; Lulu, the effervescent teenager from Dennistoun, who paved the way for a veritable chart invasion of swinging Glasgow pop stars, and Stanley Baxter, the man of a thousand faces and voices.

Francie and Josie – otherwise Jack Milroy and Rikki Fulton – who proved that comedy can span the generations, when they attracted packed houses to a theatre revival of Glasgow's gallus duo.

And any mention of the Glasgow greats would be incomplete without Billy Connolly, a product of the humour of the streets. Arguably, the Big Yin is today the best known – certainly on an international basis – of the city's stars.

The common bond between all these entertainers is that when they held centre stage they were aware, as only a Glaswegian can be, that they were – to quote a line from actress and singer Elaine C. Smith – 'pure dead brilliant'.

That brilliance shines as strongly as ever... thanks to the abundance of fresh talent which continues to spring from the city.

Thanks to the dominance of Simple Minds, Wet Wet Wet, Hue and Cry and Texas, it seems as though Glasgow's taken over the pop charts. The television scene is just as impressive. At one time the television moguls in London tended to look down their noses at the industry north of the border. Today they have to sit up and take notice.

BBC Scotland's Glasgow-based comedy unit has produced *City Lights* and *Naked Video* – which, in addition to being small screen successes, have meant stardom for young talents like Gregor Fisher, Gerard Kelly, Elaine C. Smith, Jonathan Watson, Andy Gray and Tony Roper.

The Beeb's *Tutti Frutti* series deservedly swept the boards at the BAFTA Awards – Britain's Television Oscars. My only carp is that there was no prize for the series uncredited star, Glasgow itself. The city played as vital a role as the brilliant script of John Byrne and the stunning performances of one of the best casts ever assembled in Glasgow.

Meanwhile Scottish Television did their bit to put Glasgow on the television map with their award-winning crime series, *Taggart*.

And, on the bigger screen, Glasgow's young bucks have also made an impact. John Gordon Sinclair and Clare Grogan hit the target in films directed by Bill Forsyth, who has gone on to success in Hollywood, and Peter Capaldi was among the acclaimed cast of the Oscar-winning *Dangerous Liaisons*.

The city's shooting stars will continue to shine brightly. Glasgow can be proud of them as it sees many of them back in town for another curtain call in 1990. →

Here's our line in culture

At last, Glasgow is gaining just recognition as one of Europe's leading cities.

And as one of Europe's leading companies, British Telecom is proud to be a Prime Sponsor of Glasgow 1990. We're helping to host and run the Scottish International Piano Competition — and supporting a concert in aid of two charities for the handicapped.

The Scottish Youth Theatre has turned to us too, for help in the commissioning and production of a new children's play on communication. Our funding is also encouraging up-and-coming writers. We're introducing a new initiative with the Scottish Youth Theatre's Playwright Competition. And we're also involved with the community play "City".

The field of education hasn't been forgotten either. In association with the University of Strathclyde, we're sponsoring the John Logie Baird Exhibition and there will be a schools' competition to produce a '1990' Phonecard design.

Naturally, the festival organisers are also relying on British Telecom for their telecommunications.

When Glasgow 1990 asked for our help, British Telecom in the West of Scotland answered the call.

British TELECOM
It's you we answer to

a night out – with Denis Lawson

CHRIS DOLAN

Denis Lawson
*Glasgow born.
Star in BBC's
The Justice Game.*

*We can be rather more
sophisticated than we're often
portrayed – we don't rush about
in kilts…*

*…there are dedicated,
talented people there trying to
make film and television.*

Speeding south to London, on my way to interview Denis Lawson, I bumped into Paddy Higson and Jim Gillespie, a producer and a director who have both remained in Scotland to work.

'Do stage and screen actors, like Lawson, Bill Patterson or Tom Conti have to leave Scotland to achieve their potential?'

'Yes, but things are beginning to change. Not only actors, but writers and directors are beginning to come back — or are at least spending more time working in Scotland.'

Denis Lawson echoed, from his London base, many of the views expressed by his fellow professionals. He himself is one of those actors who has returned increasingly over the years to perform or to film in Scotland. He worked with Bill Forsyth in *Local Hero*, and more recently, he played the central role of Rossi in the television series: *The Justice Game* and *The Lady from Rome*.

'Both characters portray a very contemporary kind of Scot. They break down a lot of clichés about Scottish men. We can be rather more sophisticated than we're often portrayed – we don't rush about in kilts and wellies all the time.'

I had arranged to meet Denis in a place near his home, which I understood was called The Italian Isis. Very theatrical, I thought – sounds expensive. In fact it turned out to be a small, pleasant café which sold 'Italian ices' – similar to any you would find in Glasgow.

He is a very genial and courteous man who talks earnestly about his profession, answering questions with slow deliberate precision.

'I can't help but think that our business – theatre, television, film – has been seriously damaged in the last ten years or so. We've been starved of funding. Yet it's clear that with just a

comparatively small amount of financial backing the film industry, for example, could make an incredible return – as well as producing real quality cinema.'

…specialize in that dry, ironic throwaway humour, the kind of lines that you're not sure are meant to be funny, but make you laugh anyway.

'In Australia's case, a few years ago when they were investing a lot of money in films, they not only produced first rate movies, and made a profit for the funders, but they changed the way we look at Australia now. Gone are all the old prejudices, now we think of Australia as being a vibrant, modern country.

'You can't really talk about a Scottish film industry. There is an industry only in so far as there are dedicated, talented people there trying to make films and television. There isn't even a British film industry anymore.'

He is not, however, pessimistic. '1992, and the single European market looks interesting. There are a lot of developments which make the future look bright for the business. Maybe we'll soon be in a position to talk about a European film and television industry. I hope so.'

Discussing the question of finance, European and American, brought him to musing about the cultural similarities between Glasgow and the United States.

'I've always been struck by the parallels, particularly with New York. I remember my father saying that when he was young in the late 1920s and 1930s a lot of his friends had developed trans-atlantic accents because they spent so much of their lives at the movies! But it's not just the influence of films – Glaswegian culture is much too strong for that. Both cities tend to be →

very gritty and working class in their style. You feel that in their theatre, too. Both specialize in that dry, ironic throwaway humour, the kind of lines that you're not sure are meant to be funny, but make you laugh anyway. A lot of my early influences are American – Buster Keaton, Danny Kaye, Jerry Lewis. I like working-class vaudeville; Glasgow's always done that kind of thing well.

'Peter Riebert when he was in Scotland shooting Local Hero told me that the kids in the film – John Gordon Sinclair, Peter Capaldi – were very New York in their energy and humour.

'You can't escape the resemblance. A few years ago, I did a play about the life of Lenny Bruce. He would have gone down well in Glasgow. Billy Connolly gets away with worse these days!

'Glasgow's theatre, like its culture and language, is very muscular; so is its approach to drama and audiences. Example: Years ago I was working at the The Close, which was part of the Citizen's Theatre. We were doing an adaptation of Nathanial West's A Cool Million in which David Hayman was assassinated at the end of the play. We were performing it in Amsterdam in a students union, while the bar was serving free drink. We ploughed through this horrendous experience, playing a heavy satire on American capitalism – very black, very funny – to about three hundred backs. About half way through one of the cast – a Glaswegian – just walked up to David and shot him and we went home. No mucking about.

'You get that approach in a lot of Scottish writing. John Brown, who wrote The Justice Game and The Lady from Rome has that sinewy element. It's very noir, Glaswegian but with that New York edge. It's a style that lends itself not just to pacey stories, but to political writing as well. Scotland has produced some fine politicized drama.'

I described to Denis a project which Jim Gillespie had been talking to me about the previous night. With a script by James Kelman, the Glasgow writer nominated for the Booker prize last year, and directed by Jim, it is the story of a young man's life in Drumchapel – dealing directly with drug abuse, housing conditions, all the elements of life in a working-

class scheme. The idea, outlined in a treatment by Kelman, was presented next to paintings and photographs not just from Glasgow but from Europe and America as well. Gillespie had emphasized that the film's approach is positive. 'There is', the Glasgow director had explained 'a sense of space and light in a place like Drumchapel, a view of the world which well merits exploring.'

Lawson agreed that we can only hope that works like this – contemporary and uncontrite – find favour from the money men, and help construct a genuine Scottish expression.

Denis Lawson would be happy to wrestle with the problems of his profession all day, eulogizing the colleagues he admires who are active in Scotland.

'There is a London audience and a Glasgow audience. One is as sophisticated as the other. Look at Peter Brook's The Mahabharata for example. If a producer of that calibre sees Glasgow as a cultural centre for his work, then you're going places. Look at the agenda for theatre and performance art during 1990. There are a lot of eyes on Glasgow right now. Quite rightly. I'll certainly be there.'

There is a sense of space and light in a place like Drumchapel, a view of the world which well merits exploring.

MARCH

before returning to the Royal Scottish Academy of Music and Drama in August.

Royal Opening and International Gala

2 MAR
CITY CHAMBERS
THEATRE ROYAL

The official handover from Paris — European Cultural Capital 1989 to Glasgow will take place in the presence of Her Majesty the Queen, who is the Royal Patron of Glasgow 1990.
A special celebratory international gala performance will be mounted to mark the occasion. Along with Scottish Opera and Scottish Ballet, appearing will be guest artists from the Paris Opera Ballet, La Scala Milan, the Bolshoi Ballet, the Spanish National Ballet, New York City Ballet and the Royal Ballet, Covent Garden.

Freaks

3 TO 10 MAR
TRAMWAY

Based upon the classic Tod Browning silent film of the same name, **Freaks** tells the moving story of the love of one of the so-called circus freaks for the beautiful trapeze artist, who is played by the director of the work, Genevieve de Kermabon. This powerful production is mounted by an extraordinary company from France, the majority of whom are disabled.

European Indoor Athletic Championships

3 TO 4 MAR
KELVIN HALL

Glasgow stages the 1990 European Indoor Athletic Championships this month. It's a major coup for the city, made possible by the new international facilities offered by the Kelvin Hall. World class athletes from all over Europe will compete in a full compass of events. And the edge of the →

getting physical

Image by
Alan Gallacher
Graduate, Glasgow School of Art, now freelance illustrator.

KENNY DALGLISH

Article by
©**Kenny Dalglish**
Holder of record number of Scottish caps, Liverpool's first player-manager.

One of the greatest things about Glasgow is its parks – there are plenty of green places.

Everybody in and around Glasgow lives close to a park and so there is always a chance to practise your sport. As children, fitness did not really enter our minds: it was football, football and more football.

Now, when I return to Glasgow, I can see that facilities have improved immensely and that children and grown-ups now have a far wider choice of sport. In addition there are more distractions. We did not have to contend with videos, computer games or any of the other things which tend to keep children indoors these days. The main attraction for myself and my friends was football.

During 1990 there will be a great deal of new sport coming to Glasgow. This can only have good results. It will raise people's awareness of sports other than those which they currently enjoy and therefore the possibility of making more people conscious of their health is increased.

It is very rewarding to see so many young people turning to sport and having these chances to experiment and experience new sports, but I do have a word of warning. To anyone getting involved in a new sport I would say: TAKE ADVICE.

One of the benefits of the revitalization of Glasgow is that there are more and more facilities available and, with them, many more trainers who are there to help and encourage the newcomer. In community centres and sports clubs you can meet and talk to experienced and professional people whose job it is to make sure you get the best out of the sport. They can advise you about training, equipment, facilities and fitness. I would say to anyone taking up a new sport: make use of these people. They were not there in my day.

Attitudes have changed towards sport and fitness. Health and fitness now have a far higher priority in our lives than formerly. The sport included in the programme for the Cultural Capital of Europe in Glasgow will, I am sure, further increase the awareness of fitness as an important part of modern life. As a result of the 1990 celebrations I look forward to a much healthier Glasgow (and a much healthier Liverpool!)

There is volleyball, cross-country, tug-of-war, the lot! And, of course, there is the Special Olympics. The inclusion of the Special Olympics is something which will light up the entire year and make Glasgow a very special place to be.

Further increase the awareness of fitness as an important part of modern life.

'Ordaines ane intimatioune to be on Sunday next in the respective churches that theis who keepes not the kirkis will be most severlie punished.' **(16 August 1673)**

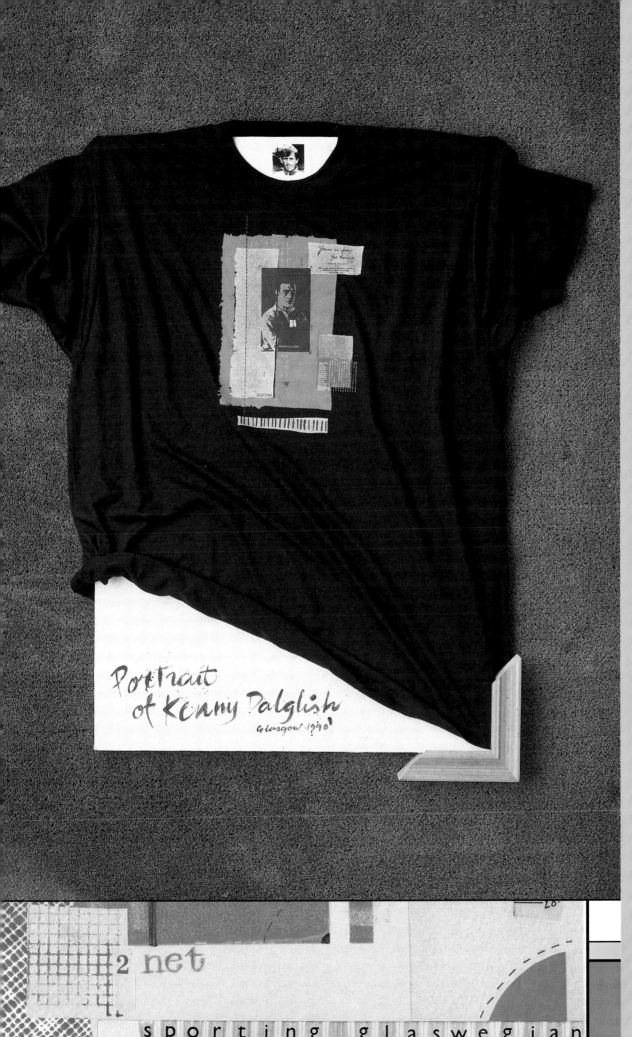

MARCH

British contingent will have been sharpened by the Commonwealth Games in Auckland earlier in the year.

UK World Cross Country Championship Trials

10 MAR
BELLAHOUSTON PARK

To add to an extremely athletic month in 1990, the selection of the British team for the UK World Cross Country Championship Trials takes place at Bellahouston Park on Saturday 10 March. The event is being held in the city as a tribute to the Centenary of the Scottish Cross Country Union.

BAFTA Craft Awards

10 TO 11 MAR
BBC
GLASGOW FILM THEATRE

The British Academy of Film and Television Arts will be hosting the annual Craft Awards in Glasgow, to be broadcast by the BBC on 11 March. The previous day there will be screenings, seminars and opportunities to meet film-makers, designers and personalities whose work has been nominated.

Steven Campbell

10 MAR TO 15 APR
THIRD EYE CENTRE

Steven Campbell is one of the most successful Scottish artists of the new generation. The Third Eye Centre is staging his first one-man show in Glasgow. Campbell has exhibited internationally since 1984. He now has paintings in the collections of museums and galleries such as The Metropolitan, The Tate Gallery and the Art Institute of Chicago. After a period spent studying in the USA, Campbell has been living and working in his native Glasgow since 1987. This show is a unique opportunity to see his new enigmatic canvasses.

2 net

sporting glaswegian

growing up

GLASGOW SCHOOLS

The views of young Glaswegians are the most authentic expression of the city. Here they describe where they live and where they play.

Oh, we do like to be

beside the seaside......!!

Infant Class. Children with severe learning difficulties, Hampden School.

'Many people have memories of living in a tenement. All the children played familiar games like tying doors in the close together, or ringing folks' bells. Then there were street games like rounders, ball games, peever, jorries, and kiss-cuddle-and-torture.' **Pauline O'Hagan, Fourth Year, St Mungo's.**

'**Even the seemingly permanent drizzle cannot dampen Glasgow's sparkle. This commercial, industrial and artistic capital talks to you with all the wit of its belligerent and boisterous people.'** Pauline O'Hagan.

Glasgow Coat of Arms. Senior Class with severe learning difficulties. Hampden School.

'My favourite place in Glasgow is the Transport Museum. It has always had old trams, bikes and prams, but nowadays it also has miniature boats, big cars, and the latest technology in hoovers and washing machines. The best of all is the old street – it is magnificent. It has a pharmacy, the picture house, a butcher, a baker, a hat shop and a camera shop. Best of all is the station, and the fancy first and second class trains.' **Louise McLaughlin, Third year, St Mungo's.**

Brian Smith, teacher at Hampden
School for children with severe
learning difficulties relates
conversations and stories from the
children at this special primary school:

'What does Glasgow mean to you?'
'Dougrie Road' said William.
'Naw! The forge' said Harriet.
'Ah live in Queen Elizabeth Square'
said Colin.
'That's the Gorbals' someone said.
'Where's the Gorbals?'
'That's where ah live' said Colin.

When three of the pupils at Hampden
School won Duke of Edinburgh Awards,
they went to the City Chambers to be
presented with their medals by Susan
Baird, the Lord Provost.

Afterwards, when they entered the
Council Chambers one of the award-
winning pupils, Theresa, sat down in
the Lord Provost's chair at the head of
the chamber, looked around
imperiously and announced: 'I feel so
important!'

Another true story concerns one of our
pupils who loved courtroom dramas on
television, and Perry Mason in
particular.

One day, he was taken to Holy
Communion in school. The normal
procedure would have been to
approach the altar, and kneel down to
receive Communion. However, on this
day, the young lad stood bolt upright
with his hands on the altar rails, waited
until the priest approached and said
very seriously in a booming voice 'NOT
GUILTY, YOUR HONOUR!'

Nadeem Moghul. Senior Class. Hampden School.

Deborah Rowantree. Primary 4, St Marnock School.

'My ancestors made
Glasgow and created its
spirit. We're the future of
Glasgow and already
we're catching that spirit
because we know that
Glasgow is *our* city, by
the way!' **James
Docherty, Fourth year,
St Mungo's.**

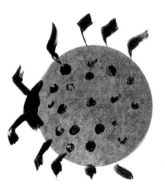

Infant Class (a combined effort).
Hampden School.

heel to heel and toe to toe

CHRIS DOLAN

Article by
Chris Dolan

Head of Media for
Network Scotland
and freelance
writer.

1961: June 30, the Queen visits
seventy-one Sandyfaulds Street
in the Gorbals, an occasion
which lives on in Glaswegian
folk memory – 'Lookit the state
a' this hoose! Whit if the Queen
wis tae walk in?'
(Glasgow Herald, 30 June 1961).

…ballet rarely manifests itself
in an identifiably national way.

International dancers make Scottish Ballet fluent in a universal art – mixing the home-grown with imports.

'Movement is a universal language – it recognizes no national boundaries', declares Lloyd Embleton, an Australian dancing with The Scottish Ballet. His colleague, Kristin Johnstone, is an American in Glasgow who finds her adopted city stimulating, but agrees that ballet rarely manifests itself in an identifiably national way.

However, The Scottish Ballet in its 1989 season staged the popular *La Sylphide*. Set in Scotland, it's a very Scottish, even Celtic, tale of forest spirits, dream and witchcraft, yet it is essentially an international creation.

The ballet was originally created by a Frenchman, August Bournonville; the music (by Herman Lovenskjold) is Danish; the leading man is danced in some performances by a South African (Vincent Hantam), in others by an English dancer (Robert Hampton); the sylph of the title is danced by Judy Mohekey from New Zealand, and by Noriko Ohara from Japan; other important members of the cast are Australian, Italian, American, Spanish and, yes, Scottish.

Another performer to dance in *La Sylphide*, Catarina Lappin, is a nineteen-year-old from East Kilbride, who has achieved a notable double first: trained at The Dance School of Scotland at Knightswood Secondary, Scotland's only school to offer ballet training alongside the normal comprehensive curriculum, Catarina is their first outstanding success.

At sixteen years old, and having finished her 'O' Levels, Catarina was offered a place at the Royal Ballet School. Within eighteen months she had a contract to dance with the National Ballet of Portugal. She loved Lisbon, but always hankered after home. After a year in Portugal, Catarina was brought back home by The Scottish Ballet.

Celebrating its twenty-first birthday in 1990, The Scottish Ballet has brought off a prodigious programme of international events. A new version of *The Knight of the Tiger Skin*, by Alexei Matchavariani has been created for them by Oleg Vinogradov, Artistic Director of the Kirov Ballet. At the same time The Scottish Ballet look westwards with the staging of two ballets originally created by George Balanchine for the New York City Ballet. The distinctive styles of these works underline the importance of Scottish Ballet's unique position in international dance. Glasgow is the privileged witness to the converging of ballet techniques from East and West. →

PROUD TO BE PART OF

GLASGOW 1990
CULTURAL CAPITAL OF EUROPE

PRIME SPONSOR

Working for "GLASGOW 1990" and beyond

As a company that's always been deeply involved in the local community, it's only natural that we should be supporting Glasgow's Year of Culture celebrations. Not that our commitment to the community will end in 1990 – we're already planning for the years beyond . . .

THE DOME

GLASGOW DOME OF DISCOVERY

March 1990 will see the South Rotunda, Govan transformed to a "hands-on" science and technology exhibition – "The Dome of Discovery." As major sponsors of this project, we're liaising with the Govan Initiative and Strathclyde Regional Council in setting up a training scheme to assist with the refurbishment and operation of the "Dome."

We're also working to help:
"The Arts is Magic," Scottish Opera, the Scottish National Orchestra and the European Special Summer Olympic Games.

A major commitment to Glasgow 1990... 1991... 1992...

BP EXPLORATION

MARCH

Arts Without Frontiers

14 TO 16 MAR
SCOTTISH EXHIBITION & CONFERENCE CENTRE/ FORUM HOTEL

The impact of the 1992 European Community single market on industry and commerce has been much debated. Now, for the first time, attention turns to the arts. At the initiative of the Arts Council of Great Britain and with the collaboration of The Sunday Times and the British Council, some 600 delegates from around the world will examine every facet of what is one of the fastest growing businesses around.

John Brown's Body

19 MAR TO 21 APR
TRAMWAY

In January 1989 the old Museum of Transport was reopened as Tramway. The inaugural production of Border Warfare was produced by Wildcat Stage Productions and directed by John McGrath. It attracted capacity audiences and was filmed for television. **John Brown's Body** follows up the theme and ideas of Border Warfare. Like its precursor, this production will exploit the vastness of the building with a large and mostly Scottish company. It will be filmed for Channel 4.

British Volleyball Championships

31 MAR TO 1 APR
KELVIN HALL

Glasgow hosts the Men's British Volleyball Championships. This is the first time for several seasons that Scotland will have played at home. Recently, a British men's team was created, and this event offers a rare opportunity for players to catch the eye of the new Great Britain coach. Of course, the championships will enthral enthusiasts. But they also provide a chance for sports fans and the athletically curious →

And for Catarina the young Scottish dancer who started her career in Glasgow, is there, amidst all this inter-continental activity, anything fundamentally Glaswegian about dancing in Glasgow?

She agrees with Lloyd and Kristin that ballet is a human discipline which transcends country of

origin. But to her dancing in Glasgow *is* different, *is* important. In one sense it's a personal thing: her family and friends can relate much more easily to her art now that she's back home. They see the posters, read the reviews, actually go to all the performances – but there is also the nature of Glasgow as a city.

heel to heel and toe to toe

NEIL WALLACE

**Article by
Neil Wallace**
Deputy Director of the Festivals Office; a director of Scottish Ballet.

…a focus for the creation and discussion of new work…

…outstanding international artists can perform here, making Glasgow second only to London…

As it happens, contemporary dance is one of the first highlights to open the year. Throughout January, February and March, we'll be seeing the biggest New Moves season ever from the Third Eye Centre. This festival of the newest dance and choreography from Britain and further afield is only three years old, but it's becoming the most important British platform of its kind after Dance Umbrella in London. It's a focus for the creation and discussion of new work, not just a chance to watch it. A showcase for younger choreographers, at least six of whom will be part of the programme. Lloyd Newson and Nigel Charnock of DV8 will be in residence, beginning preliminary work on a new, large-scale piece to be created for Tramway later this summer and produced in association with two major French dance festivals in Rouen and Montpellier. Liz Rankin, Wendy Houstoun, Rosemary Lee, Stephanie Bowyer, Sue Smith, Virginia Farman, Sian Thomas, the Martins Gent and Cole, will all première short pieces. Internationally, New Moves welcomes David Dorfman's company from New York, at least one group from Holland. But pride of place in Nikki Milican's 1990 New Moves programme for me will be *Giant*, the new work from Scotland's leading contemporary company, the Gregory Nash Dance Group. It is Greg's first full-length piece for four years. It has some of my favourite dancers in it, and it opens at Tramway – a space which has already proved its credentials for dance (pillars and all). In June, Glasgow's

Rotating Dancers will use one of the long galleries for a new piece there.

There will be the Mayfest dance programme, an outstanding success last year and sure to bring some of the most exciting companies in Europe to Glasgow. During the summer Nederlands Dans Theater 2 will be back to the Theatre Royal following its 1988 visit. NDT is quite simply one of the best young contemporary companies anywhere in the world, but it won't be the only world-class company in Glasgow in 1990 by any means. We'll see a return by Anne Teresa de Keersmaeker. Rosemary Butcher Dance Company will première a completely new work for the city commissioned by Third Eye. And of course there are companies and groups still on the shortlist for later in the year – in other words surprises still to come.

Even five years ago, a dance programme of this distinction just couldn't have taken place in Glasgow. It's a tribute to New Moves, to Mayfest and to the Theatre Royal that such outstanding international artists can perform here, making Glasgow second only to London in the number and quality of performances the dance audience can see. But it's only the beginning for our own dance artists and choreographers and *their* creative aspirations. That's the post 1990 challenge.

The distinctive styles of these works underline the importance of Scottish Ballet's unique position in international dance.

**Image by
Alistair Hall**

'Glasgow is just simply a wonderful, vibrant city'.

MARCH

to see this fast-growing and action-packed sport played to the highest standard.

UK Comics Convention

31 MAR TO 1 APR
CITY CHAMBERS

Throughout the convention, a host of comic creators from home and abroad will talk about their work and sign autographs for fans. The brilliant Mexican cartoonist Sergio Aragones best known for his anarchic contributions to Mad Magazine will be there. Also coming are writers and artists from Marvel Comics, DC and representatives from Two Thousand AD. There will be exhibitions of original art work. Thousands of comics and related items will be on sale. There's a charity auction and fancy dress contests. Everyone who turns up will take away a special souvenir booklet marking the convention.

Scottish National Festival of Youth Theatre

31 MAR TO 8 APR
ROYAL SCOTTISH ACADEMY OF MUSIC & DRAMA

With indigenous young people from Ayr to Angus, and with invited groups from as far apart in geography and lifestyle as Istanbul and Oslo, the Scottish National Youth Theatre is staging its third annual festival in Glasgow. This year they hope to have more than twenty groups presenting the fruits of their thespian labours over nine days.

the Glasgow collections

N O R M A N   M A C F A R L A N E

Article by
Norman
MacFarlane
*Kt 1982 for services
to Industry and the
Arts.*

*I was approached recently by
four lady visitors who told
me that they had been to the
art galleries. Burrell, the
Hunterian and the Transport
Museums all of which they
had found interesting.
However, the friendliness
they had encountered during
their short stay had given
them an appetite to see and
feel more of Glasgow so
discarding the set tour I took
them firstly to the People's
Palace, through the Gorbals,
to Kings Park and into
Castlemilk where they spent
some time in a community
centre tearoom and met a
lady who invited them to visit
her fourteenth floor flat in
the estate 'to see the view'.*
**Hugh MacNaughton, Taxi
Driver.**

**Although Sir William Burrell was the most important of the
industrialist collectors associated with Glasgow, he was by
no means the only one.**

There have been, and still are, many others, commencing with Archibald
McLellan, the Glasgow coachbuilder and city magistrate, whose
collection was gifted to Glasgow and formed the basis of the great
municipal collections we now enjoy.

McLellan's pictures included many important old masters, but the jewel in
the crown which is still the star of Glasgow's collections was Giorgione's
The Adultress brought before Christ.

The Reid brothers of the North British Locomotive Company, which was at
one time the largest engineering shop in Europe, were knowledgeable and
enthusiastic collectors. They gave the Glasgow gallery Corot's Pastorale
among other items. The Cargill family of Burmah Oil, the Teacher family of
whisky fame, the Coats thread family, Smillie, Chrystal and others
collected wisely and were generous to their local gallery.

For me, the most interesting and exciting Glasgow collection, excepting
Burrell, was created by William McInnes, who like so many of his fellow
collectors in the west of Scotland was involved in shipping.

McInnes was different from the others in many ways. He was not wealthy
by their standards and lived in a modest flat on the south side of Glasgow.
He was a bachelor and apart from his business had only two real
interests, paintings and music. Leslie Hunter, one of the Scottish Colourist
painters became a close friend of McInnes and this association played an
important part in the creation of the collection. It was absolutely
necessary for McInnes to love a painting before he would consider its
acquisition, and a visit to his flat where he was surrounded by his
treasures was a joy for his friends. Slowly at first but with great
deliberation, McInnes developed a standard of taste which is clearly
reflected in his collection.

When he died in 1944 his entire collection was bequeathed to Glasgow Art
Gallery. To many people's amazement it consisted of over one hundred
paintings and etchings, among which were works by Monet, Renoir,
Cézanne, Van Gogh, Sisley, Degas, Fantin-Latour, Bonnard, Vuillard,
Braque, Picasso, Matisse and other internationally acclaimed painters,
as well as outstanding works by leading Scottish artists. →

Image by
Clare Melinsky
*Illustrator using
lino cuts. Lives near
Sanquhar,
Dumfriesshire.*

The Glasgow Collection "City of Culture 1990"   Clare Melinsky '89

APRIL

American Football

APR TO MAY

HELENVALE PARK

The entire coaching squad of Simon Fraser University, founded by a Scot, is coming to show us American Football as it should be. It will be conducting coaching seminars for kids and for coaches. Players won't be confined to the stage during this tour!

Henry Moore Exhibition

APR TO OCT

POLLOK PARK

From April to October, a unique chance to see Henry Moore's work in a perfect setting – the open fields of Pollok Park. The works – nine large bronzes in all – will be sited next to the Burrell Collection, making Pollok Park a double attraction over the spring, summer and autumn. The pieces have been lent and selected by the Henry Moore Foundation and embody familiar themes: mother and child, the female figure and form, and the family.

Writing Together

3 TO 7 APR

GLASGOW UNIVERSITY

In September 1989, **Writing Together**, a major three-part international writers' project, opened in Glasgow. This month sees the second part. And the final part will take place in September.

The project brings together published writers from every continent and involves them with one another and with people from all over the city.

Events include readings, competitions, various writers' workshops, storytelling sessions, and meetings with women's and ethnic groups. There will also be public readings, public discussion of key issues and trends in world fiction, and some specialist conferences and book exhibitions.

Two Americans discovered the Glasgow traditional 'hauf and hauf' and decided in their glow of happiness that they could not return home without seeing Loch Lomond. As they had an hour before their train, they hailed a taxi. They were both nearly sleeping before the taxi had moved off. The driver knew there was insufficient time, but not wishing to disappoint his passengers, drove around the city for fifteen minutes finally arriving at the much smaller Hogganfield Loch. He woke the happy pair who after squinting through the window in the dim light declared themselves suitably impressed!

Hugh MacNaughton

Why should so many industralist collectors arise so regularly in this city? It is a unique phenomenon, geographically and artistically. What was, and still is, so special about Glasgow which created the ambience in which the industrialist collector of intelligence and genuine erudition flourished?

The major factor almost certainly is the existence in Glasgow of two old established artistic institutions.

The first, the Royal Glasgow Institute of the Fine Arts, was a major success from the time it was established in 1861. It organized a large, highly selective, annual exhibition of professional standard, and provided an outlet for the emerging creative talents of the Glasgow painters. These were the young men who, in the 1880s, blossomed into the Glasgow School of Painters, or the Glasgow Boys, as they preferred to call themselves.

The other arts organization which played a notable part in creating the environment which allowed talent to flourish was the Glasgow Art Club. It was from its start in 1867 a small club of great character, dominated by artists who found in its warm, hospitable, almost bohemian atmosphere, a welcome haven from their labours in their neighbouring studios. The club, as might be expected of a hostelry run by artists had more than its share of friction, financial storms, and great moments, but it never suffered from apathy!

The Glasgow Institute and the Art Club have each, with a few ups and downs, flourished. They have in their different ways provided a wonderful opportunity for artists and laymen to congregate, discuss, exhibit, educate, and generally benefit from each other's company.

This close and intimate relationship between artists and industrialists, created an environment in Glasgow which stimulated the interest and instincts of wealthy businessmen to collect not only the work of their painter friends, but also to be advised by them as to what they should purchase from artists in other countries.

Does the same artistic atmosphere still exist in Glasgow today? A visit to the city will prove that it does, and that the influence of Charles Rennie Mackintosh, the Glasgow Boys, the Institute, the Art Club, Burrell, McInnes, and many other creative factors are still present in Glasgow, making it the most exciting and stimulating artistic environment in Britain today.

Extracts from an article published in Britoil Magazine 87/88.

the Glasgow collections

ALASTAIR BURNET

**Article by
Alastair Burnet**

Kt 1984; Broadcaster and writer, worked on Glasgow Herald, 1951-58.

From the years when no one thought too much of, or with, or for, Glasgow, to the year in which Glasgow is the Cultural Capital of Europe, is possibly a very long step for some, but only a short one for some of the rest of us.

We are all subject to the associations of our own past. We thought Glasgow underrated (but then, weren't many things in Scotland rightly underrated, as time has shown?) So I'm wholly and all the more delighted now, though not surprised, that it is being given a prominence and a recognition that it has earned the hard

way, and probably deserves the hard way, but which some of our people and our friends have been the first to dispute and deny.

The Glasgow which I adopted as my home town in the 1930s was a murky place, now beset in memory by rolling fogs (which justified the invention of the tramcar) and by a steady smirr of rain, which never seemed to move more than a hundred yards away even when the sun was out and momentarily attacked the dampness of the close. But it was then, and still is in my elderly mind, the Second City of the Empire. →

Although we all know better than that nowadays, it was not an idle matter then. I think it helped to see Glasgow through a slump and a war, and, after all, such was our intellectual contribution to the empire, we did have four daily newspapers (and the Noon Record) and three evenings, so that the disparaging idea of internal colonialism, which Michael Hechter was to put forward in 1975 (far cleverer than any Scottish Nationalist), could not have been imagined in the 1950s when we sub-editors on the stone exchanged our influential night's work on the early morning trams.

I have never seen Glasgow in any other light than that. I am a child of its superior, self-confident years. My grandparents lived in Hillhead Street in the 1930s (No 60 and then No 52; now both, I think, in the maw of the university) and it was natural that, as Carlyle's statue watched the start and finish of every compulsory childhood walk in Kelvingrove Park, I should have to read and admire the author of *Sartor Resartus* and *Past and Present*.

And then there was the Art Gallery. (I remember, when I worked on the *Herald,* what a great stramash there was when the town council changed the department's name from Art Gallery and Museums to Museums and Art Gallery.) When I go back now it's ineradicably overlaid with reminiscence, but I count myself fortunate to have been brought up on what percipient people had bought for the Impressionist room and, more than that, to have seen McTaggart's Paps of Jura and the Galloway Landscape and the Peploes and the others that taught me to recognize what I wasn't wrong to like. I remember, as if it were yesterday, going to see an exhibition of J. D. Fergusson's in Sauchiehall Street and coming out into the rain with eyes trained (even for a short while) to the mystery and wonder of colour.

Of course, in my day we didn't have Scottish Opera or Ballet, and even the Scottish National Orchestra had to be supported in even more strenuous leading articles. But Glasgow's musical tradition, a sturdy one, drew its resilience from away back in Victorian times. It always seemed, and still seems, to me a hardier one than some other festival occasions.

And then there are the writers. Glasgow is admired now for its Victorian buildings, the buildings we used to take for granted. I happen to think that eyes brought up on George Square, or Greek Thomson or the terraces of the west end or the mansions of Pollokshields were given, however haphazardly, a sense of proportion, of congruity, of taste even, to measure later efforts. But I don't think Glasgow's Victorian and post-Victorian novelists and other writers have been given the same reappraisal.

To me, many of Sherlock Holmes's cases actually happened along the Great Western Road; to me, Tempe and the dales (or is it better as vales?) of Arcady are somewhere around Bellahouston Park, where my grandmother and mother took me to the Empire Exhibition in 1938. But put that aside. We knew, all those years ago, that we were living in a green and amiable and satisfying – and restless and original – place.

Good. That's Glasgow. That's us, and that's our friends. I don't doubt that in this promotion year for the Jags (look us up under P for Partick) there'll be some of us who will have doubts and reservations to the last. As for me I'm content that almost everywhere I look in the city the trendy people have had to catch up.

Alan Arneil

APRIL

Writing Together aims to stimulate discussion about language, nationhood, class, gender, race and culture – and to interest and involve the public in these discussions.

Glasgow's Glasgow

13 APR TO 5 DEC
CENTRAL STATION 'ARCHES' MIDLAND STREET

Glasgow's Glasgow (The Words and the Stones) is a central focus of the 1990 programme. It interprets the 1,000 year history of Glasgow in a thoroughly exciting and innovative way.

The exhibition will be staged in twenty-two massive brick-vaulted arches below Central Station, a space unknown and unvisited for two generations. Thousands of objects associated with the city and its story will be displayed. Theatrical performances, songs, film and video will inhabit the exhibition, designed as a 'city landscape' by Glasgow's leading designers and architects.

Explore Glasgow's past, a city that was once the richest industrial centre in the world, leading the way in science, engineering, medicine and municipal government. Witness its terrible decline. And see the stirrings of its contemporary renaissance.

Glasgow's Glasgow is not to be missed, whether you know a lot or just a little about the city.

The treasures on display come from private and museum collections all over the world, including the U.S.S.R., United States, Canada, Germany and Austria. There are ship models and steam hammers, pennants and trophies, items which range from a Fabergé egg made for the Tsar of Russia to a Shanks toilet.

Within the arches there will be many exciting experiences. Fly through the city on a computer. Ride the world's first bicycle. Have fun with a science circus. Explore a Glasgow tenement. Watch Scotland score its finest goals. And in a specially created →

Image by
Heather Nevay
'I love living here.'

the music makers

NEVILLE GARDEN

Article by
Neville Garden

*Journalist and
broadcaster.
Presenter, BBC
Radio Scotland.*

Glasgow's links with the musical world are strong. The city houses the headquarters of two symphony orchestras, an internationally famed opera company, and an adventurous ballet company.

But Glasgow, in 1990, is something else. For the music lover, it represents a cornucopia overflowing with goodies. Never, surely, has a city crammed so many outstanding musical attractions into the space of one year.

Six gems are emerging from Scottish Opera, including Verdi's violent tale of vengeance *The Force of Destiny*, Richard Strauss's *Salome* (complete with Dance of the Seven Veils) and that massive work of Berlioz, *The Trojans* — which got its first complete performance in Britain at the hands of an amateur company in Glasgow back in the 1930s! It was a city of culture then, too.

What's more, Kenneth Leighton's most serenely beautiful opera *Columba* is being staged in Glasgow Cathedral. With that magical maestro Sir Alexander Gibson conducting, it should not be missed.

Some might argue that the biggest attraction of Glasgow 1990 is Pavarotti. Grandfathers speak of Caruso, fathers talk of Gigli. Pavarotti is the tenor of our time.

The huge man with the heaven sent voice is a festival in himself. Whatever he sings, be it a full-blown Verdi aria or a simple Neapolitan song, it will be sung *from* the heart and go straight *to* the heart.

Those with orchestral tastes are well served throughout the year by the 'residents' — the Scottish National Orchestra, the Scottish Chamber Orchestra and the BBC Scottish Symphony Orchestra. Their respective programmes are rewarding and often adventurous.

They are the musical cake: the icing on it is provided by a fine array of visiting orchestras. The Leipzig Gewandhaus Orchestra is especially interesting, since musicians are permitted to join only if they are related to existing members or have been taught by a member. In this way, the warm, mellow sound of the orchestra (specially created for the hall in which they play) is preserved.

The Leningrad Symphony is arguably one of the most exciting orchestras in the world. I first heard it in another Scottish city, some 50 miles to the east and could scarcely believe what I was hearing, they made the hair stand up on the back of my neck. →

. . . the icing on it is provided by a fine array of visiting orchestras.

APRIL

theatre, there will be theatre, music, ceilidhs, jazz, TV and radio shows — day and night.

Belgian Performance Season

16 TO 21 APR
THIRD EYE CENTRE

Recently, new theatre, performance and dance from Belgium have become prominent in the world of the avant-garde and experimental. The country's young artists, theatre makers and choreographers are now in great demand throughout Europe and at international festivals.

Recognizing this achievement, the Third Eye Centre presents a season of work by artists and groups working in smaller-scale spaces. Third Eye has already presented Wim Vandekuybus and his company, and collaborated to make possible the first appearance of Anne Teresa de Keersmaeker in Glasgow.

European Community Youth Orchestra

24 APR
CITY HALL

In its twelve years of innovative, creative music making the ECYO, which draws its performers from twelve EEC countries, has performed in most of the major towns, cities and festivals throughout the European Community. The programme for this concert, to be conducted by Matthias Bamert, reflects the breadth of the Orchestra's repertoire and will include the Brahms Concerto for Violin and Violincello, in which the soloists will be Salvatore Accardo and Mario Brunello.

The new Concert Hall will be host to the Berlin Philharmonic Orchestra, for so long the superb plaything of the mighty Herbert von Karajan. His death robbed the world of an emperor of the rostrum.

So the list goes on. There is early music and new music. Premières are scheduled for a series of Musica Nova concerts, which also feature music by the American John Cage. He once 'composed' a piece called '4'33"'. A pianist sits at the keyboard for exactly that duration, stands up and walks off the platform. The 'music' is whatever sounds the audience has picked up during the silence. With a bit of luck, they'll hear a bit more this time!

Harpsichord buffs are catered for, as are lovers of the 'king of instruments', the organ: and, as befits the city which gave birth to the world-famous Orpheus Choir, there is an event called Chorus International. During two weeks some of Europe's finest choral institutions will sing a staggering variety of music.

The Choir of King's College, Cambridge, for example, offers the mystical *Requiem* by Maurice Durufle, now in his eighties and a recluse whose compositions number barely a dozen. The boys' voices of this choir are among the most limpid and heart-stopping in the world. Also included are performances by Capella Nova of all five Masses composed by the forgotten genius of the Scottish Renaissance, Robert Carver.

All too much? Not a bit of it. Remember, these are only some highlights of what promises to be an amazing 12 months.

I have a feeling that in 1990 Glasgow will be on its feet — and cheering.

the Bolshoi opera from Russia with love

IAIN E. AGNEW

Article by
Iain E. Agnew

Freelance actor,
writer and
broadcaster.

When you mention the Bolshoi, everyone assumes that you're talking about the famous ballet company. Few realize that the Bolshoi Theatre in Moscow also houses a famous opera company; and the bonus is they have never visited Great Britain before. Where are they going – London or Edinburgh perhaps? No. In the summer of 1990, the Bolshoi Opera will be performing in Glasgow, Cultural Capital of Europe.

The history of the Bolshoi Theatre dates from 28 March 1776, when Prince Urusov, an *aficionado* of drama and music, was granted a concession to produce all theatrical performances in Moscow for a period of ten years. He invited an English impresario, Michael E. Maddox, to be director and they decided to build their own theatre on Petrovka Street. The Petrovsky Theatre was eventually opened on the site now occupied by the Bolshoi Theatre.

In 1842, a new dimension was added to the Bolshoi Theatre – opera. Glinka's *Ivan Susanin* appeared on stage in September of that year, followed four years later by *Russlan and Ludmilla*. These dates have become landmarks in the history of the Bolshoi. Glinka, and later Dargomizhsky, were largely responsible for the Bolshoi Opera's tenet of realism.

At the beginning of the twentieth century, the Bolshoi entered a golden age and became renowned the world over as one of the most influential music and ballet centres. The best operas in the world were to be found there. However, a threat – and challenge – to its talents lay in the aftermath of the October Revolution. Up to that point, the Bolshoi had been a closed institution, catering to a small élite – now it had to open its doors to the people. This it did to great effect. The Bolshoi is no sleeping bear – through its work, Russia's history, culture and art are given a voice – and what a mighty voice it is.

ONCE AGAIN, WE'RE

ARTIST ANTHONY ARMSTRONG

DELIGHTED TO

THE BERLIN PHILHARMONIC ORCHESTRA
PHOTO: DEUTSCHE GRAMMOPHON/LAUTERWASSER

PLAY

A SUPPORTING

PISSARRO: 'THE THRESHING MACHINE, MONTFOUCAULT'
1876. PRIVATELY OWNED

ROLE.

At The Royal Bank of Scotland we work hard to support our customers. And that means much more than just providing a sympathetic, highly efficient banking service. It means encouraging excellence in all things. So we are particularly proud to be a Prime Sponsor of Glasgow 1990 Cultural Capital of Europe. By supporting, amongst other things, the Pissarro Exhibition, the Glasgow Collection and the opening concert by the Berlin Philharmonic Orchestra we are able to play a part in applauding Glasgow.

The Royal Bank of Scotland

WHERE PEOPLE MATTER

The Royal Bank of Scotland plc. Registered Office: 36 St. Andrew Square, Edinburgh EH2 2YB. Registered in Scotland No. 90312.

playing from the heart

D A V I D   B E L C H E R

Article by
David Belcher
Writes about this rock and pop lark in the Glasgow Herald.

'The thing about Glasgow people, the Glasgow punter, is that he will listen to anything and, if it is done well, he will like it.'

Sydney Devine

As Liverpool was to British popular music in the sixties, so Glasgow would see itself being in the eighties and nineties, a seedbed for musical talent and a hothouse for achievement. Rock is the city's most recent, most apparent, most successful contribution to the performing arts, something for which Glasgow is becoming known world-wide.

Glasgow presently likes to think of itself, with a measure of statistical justification, as the most musically-productive British city of the past decade. Glasgow-domiciled bands such as Wet Wet Wet, Hue and Cry, the Blue Nile, the Silencers, the River Detectives, Gun, Hipsway, Deacon Blue, and Texas, have all, along with exiled native sons like Simple Minds, achieved notable success in charts and concert halls.

Besides these big names there are dozens of less well-known Glaswegian bands, some already signed to big labels, some desperately trying to attract their attention, jostling in the wings. Completing the process squads of record company talent-spotters, lured from their metropolitan headquarters by the city's track record, visit Glasgow with a regularity surely much envied by groups in other British cities.

Within the last ten years a fully-functioning everyday music business infrastructure of studios, venues, experienced management teams, and rehearsal rooms has arisen from what was hitherto a musical desert. Thus groups now no longer need be automatically relocated to London in order to begin their careers or further them.

So just why are there so many Glasgow bands, more bands than from any other United Kingdom city of comparable size? →

Image by
David Band

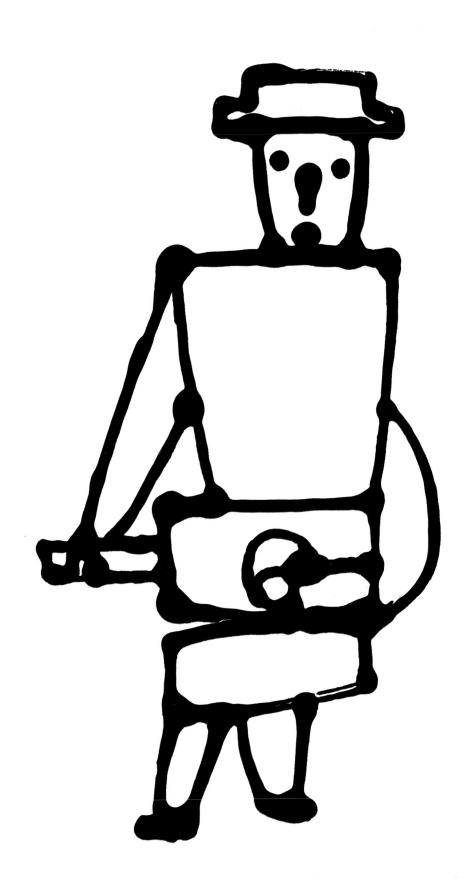

1985

John Bellany Exhibition

1 TO 31 MAY
COMPASS GALLERY

John Bellany returns with an exhibition of new paintings and watercolours. He admits to being inspired by his recent brush with death during an operation and his reinvigorated and powerful imagery – huge still-lives in a relatively Impressionistic style – fire the imagination. John is an internationally renowned artist and has received the accolade of a one man retrospective at the Gallery of Modern Art.

Mayfest

4 TO 27 MAY
CITYWIDE

The 1990 **Mayfest** programme is sure to be one of the highlights of the year. The annual festival continues to grow in size, range and quality.

Mayfest is recognized as one of Europe's key festivals for theatre, dance, music and related performing arts. But, while international in policy and style, its foundations are Scottish and it provides a platform for the best in contemporary Scottish culture.

Like many major festivals, the **Mayfest** programme is confirmed at a late stage. You'll be able to pick up the full programme in March. But once again we are sure to see interesting and surprising productions from all over the world. There will also be an outstanding cabaret, music and entertainment programme. And dozens of performances will tour, and arise from Glasgow's communities.

Front Line States – a season of anti-apartheid work by African artists and groups will be one major component of the festival.

Expect a repeat success of last year's dance programme. Mayfest is also planning a major season of theatre from Soviet Georgia, and a celebration of Celtic music.

It might sound flippant, but the chief reason could be because the young people of Europe's first self-designated post-industrial city perceive themselves as having more chance of getting on *Top of the Pops* with a number one hit record than of securing a 'proper job' as an apprentice electrician or a junior office worker.

As all along they really wanted to be Jim Kerr, rather than an electrician or an office worker, they decide they might as well try to achieve what appears to be a more-readily-attainable goal, that of global rock super stardom.

Okay so far? Yes and no. If the Glasgow connection is to remain a viable music industry one, it has to shake off the preoccupation which its bands have with sounding as though they come from somewhere else. A major problem with Glasgow bands is that they are not musically identifiable as coming from Glasgow (which, perversely, is their main unifying characteristic).

Why is this? Without getting too sociological, as representatives of a minority culture, Glaswegians have long experienced discrimination and ridicule for the very fact of being Glaswegian, for sounding different. When abroad in southern Britain, the Glaswegian felt ridiculed into modifying his speech. Until the advent of the Proclaimers (pointedly Scottish, but pointedly not from Glasgow), no one other than old unhip folkies in unstylish Arran jumpers sang in a Scottish accent.

The musical events scheduled to take place in Glasgow during 1990 will help throw the city's ideas about itself into clearer relief, and aid it in defining its own strengths and weaknesses.

New Music World, being staged at the Tramway and in performing venues and lecture theatres all over the city over five days in September, is likely to be the most important. Seen as a more couthy west of Scotland rejoinder to New York's long-established New Music Seminar, New Music World aims to bring together musicbiz scions and groovers of academe in informed and challenging discussion. Additionally, there will be live music from forward-thinking bands from around the world.

Immediately preceding New Music World there will be a three-day festival of world and traditional music. It will be based in Pollok Park, and will feature international performers, with one of its stated intentions being collaboration between the visiting musicians and players from all of Glasgow's many and varied communities.

loving the blues

JIM WAUGH

Article by
Jim Waugh
*Broadcasts and
writes on jazz.*

It was all Bill Haley's fault. If *Rock Around the Clock* had not been such a bad film and if Haley's music had not seemed so trite, shallow and pointless, I would never have discovered the glories of Bill Broonzy or John Lee Hooker or (most glorious of all) Sonny Terry.

Finding out about jazz and blues in those days of reluctant record companies was not easy. There was a branch of Collet's at Charing Cross where we could pick up Folkways records and one or two other shops gradually increased their jazz and blues bins as demand rose. Generally,

though, it was a matter of taking your chance and grabbing what you could find.

Tom McGrath, Jim Vallance, Stewart Rae and myself were running a small jazz club called The Cell. In addition to the Friday night raves we decided to open on a Sunday afternoon. We called the new venture Horizons. Tom Wright offered some poems which McGrath set and which were read in what I now discover were some of the earliest poetry and jazz sessions outside Greenwich Village. A young bass player appeared who could play more like Charles

Mingus than anyone we had heard. He was with us for a few months and then left to go to London. The next we heard from Jack Bruce was that he was joining this band called Cream.

McGrath and one or two others were trying to play free jazz at what turns out to be just about the same time as Ornette Coleman and John Coltrane were forming their double quartet plans which resulted in the shattering album called 'Free Jazz'. Then Coltrane came to Glasgow. He brought a quintet which included the wonderful Eric Dolphy. They played the St Andrew's Halls in support of Dizzy Gillespie.

Folk music was also growing up. In the mid-fifties, we had been dominated by America, and black America at that. We listened to and got the message of Huddie Ledbetter. The fact that this apparently gentle singer of the country tradition was recorded while serving his second sentence for murder added a romantic appeal. How different from our own dull home life!

Broonzy was touring, Sonny Terry and Brownie McGhee came back to Josh MacRae's flat after a gig and we played all night. Archie Fisher discovered an album by an itinerant New York eccentric called Moondog. Robert Zimmerman had not yet wangled his way into his first job as a floor sweeper with CBS Records, so Dylan was, for us, just a Welsh poet who made words dance and sing. We played the blues and were proud of it.

Then doubt began to crack our conviction. People began asking what right we had to play the music of ex-slaves, of disenfranchised second-rate citizens, the music of the down-trodden and despised. Well, we replied, we *are* Scottish.

That argument, while it had its point to make, was merely intellectual and we gradually discovered, through the likes of Norman and Janie Buchan and the wonderful Hamish Henderson, that there were songs of deprivation and despair, of anger and revolt and love in our own tradition. In many ways, of course, the lifestyle of an eighteenth-century Aberdeenshire farm labourer was just as foreign to us as the Louisiana share cropper, but at least it felt more honest.

The establishment of the Glasgow International Jazz Festival is one of the most important events in the recent history of the music in the city. For the first time, Glasgow fans and players could not only hear the very best, they could meet them for a drink after the concert, talk over attitudes and techniques and exchange that common currency of music throughout the world – the tale told tall or true.

Over the last three years I have sat in concerts with local musicians, heard them gasp in astonishment or nod in agreement with something played by a visiting American or European player. The 1990 Jazz Festival will highlight the best of European jazz and Europe has, for many years benefited from a far more organized touring network and the readiness of American musicians to settle in Europe. The 1990 Festival will open a few ears. And that is how festivals work: by stimulating local players to retire to what America calls 'the woodshed', a place where you can work out new ways of doing things. Festivals also work by making it plain that the local player is not operating in a vacuum, that there are others out there thinking along the same lines. It's a process of growing up, and over the last few years, Glasgow jazz and folk music have done a lot of growing up.

Bill Haley has a lot to answer for.

In Glasgow, we could relate the things that were talked about and sung about in the Country songs, to what was actually happening round about us. The Country songs were full of hardship and suffering. We could look around and see the same kind of hardships. But there was always a happy ending – always. So you could listen to this list of disasters knowing that there would be something good at the end – like Glasgow! Sydney Devine

Image by
Elaine Buchanan

Glasgow born and trained, now living in London trying to make a living.

street walking – the renaissance of the merchant city

ROSEMARY LONG

Article by
Rosemary Long

Evening Times senior feature writer, women's editor and columnist, winner of several Press Awards.

New life in an old city: Rosemary Long writes on the contemporary use of a major nineteenth century architectural achievement: The invasion of the derelict and unused by the imaginative and energetic.

Someone is grinding coffee at the open window of a flat in Wilson Street. The glorious message of crushed cloves of garlic wafts from the Fire Station Restaurant in Ingram Street. From the Casa Fina gift shop, subtle scents of pot pourri escape into Glassford Street, woodland and lemon, cinammon and rose petal.

'About 1750 no street lamps were lit on Sabbath evenings, and the inhabitants were prevented by the authorities from walking on the streets during the day.' **(Saint Mungo's Bells – A. J. Callant, 1888)**

In the sixteenth century, the smell near the bottom of Glasgow's High Street was the smell of animal skins being scraped and stretched and tanned. Add that to the odd bid of ordure and some pretty whiffy passers-by, and what you had was a pong of prodigious proportions. But at least things were going on, in a small, smelly, villagey sort of way. While ten years ago, what was going on at the Merchant City, it is now known, was precisely . . . zilch.

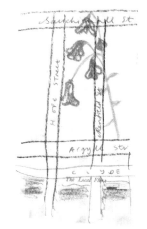

Warehouses loomed ominously over drab streets. Pieces of waste ground offered rent-free space to feral cats and their scraggy offspring. The striking black-and-glass *Daily Express* building had lain empty since the mid-seventies. The Press Bar underneath played host to a few penny-pinching students and telephone workers and sighed for the days when hard-drinking newsmen (and women!) rushed in for doubles after every edition.

Ghosts hovered over the historic Ramshorn Churchyard (as they still do)

Ghosts hovered over the historic Ramshorn Churchyard (as they still do, of course) and the Houndstitch building still housed a traditional shopping emporium, but doucely, its finest trading days long gone.

What a difference ten years makes. Good-bye gloomsville, hullo yuppieville. I was one of the very first folk to move into the Merchant City when it was still a mass of scaffolding and JCB's, wolf-whistling workmen and men in hard hats holding complicated drawings in their hands, shaking their heads and sighing at strange structural oddities thrown up by the intrusive claws of new machinery. →

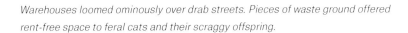

Warehouses loomed ominously over drab streets. Pieces of waste ground offered rent-free space to feral cats and their scraggy offspring.

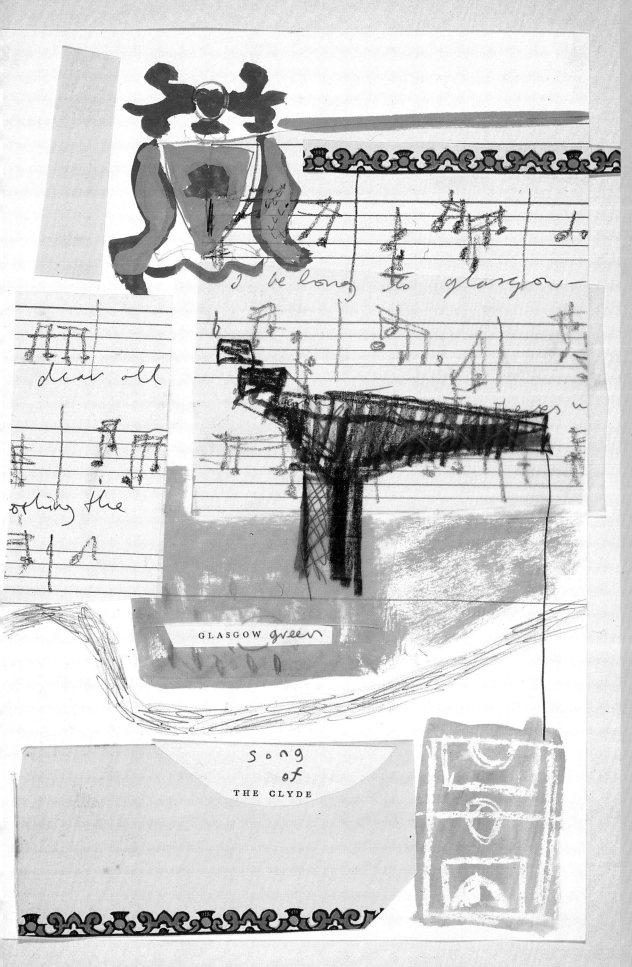

MAY

Presented by Regular Music, the city will host a week-long festival of the best in country music – new and not-so-new. Participants are likely to include the Judds, Dwight Yokum and the first British appearances of other bands from Europe as well as the USA. It'll also be a platform for Scotland's own leading country bands. Big concerts will be in one central venue, with lots of other gigs in a pub circuit. And there'll be a Festival Club in Glasgow's famous Grand Ole Opry, Paisley Road West. Other features of the New Country week will be workshops, seminars and talks for local musicians and fans.

Pavarotti

16 MAY
SCOTTISH EXHIBITION & CONFERENCE CENTRE

What can be said about Luciano Pavarotti that hasn't been said before?

This great Italian tenor has broadened the horizons of classical music and brought untold numbers of new fans to opera. His reputation is legendary, and it's fitting that he comes to Glasgow to give a special celebratory concert to help mark the city's cultural year.

Accompanied by Scottish Opera, together with flautist Andrea Griminelli, Pavarotti will sing some of the world's greatest operatic arias, a repertoire of songs which have moved countless audiences throughout the world.

The Arts is Magic

30 TO 31 MAY
SCOTTISH EXHIBITION & CONFERENCE CENTRE

For the first time in Glasgow, a festival which focuses on the integration of handicapped/disabled young individuals with their non-disabled peers and allows them to share experiences through the Arts. Around 3,000 participants are expected with all tickets being free. This is a UK first.

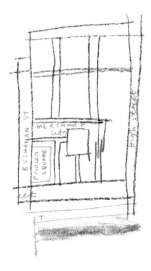

...there was a suggestion that emigrants had once huddled there with their bundles and hopes, waiting for a passage to the Dominion.

My building then was the Wimpey one in Miller Street, called grandly Canada Court, because there was a suggestion that emigrants had once huddled there with their bundles and hopes, waiting for a passage to the Dominion. I bought a drawing, not a house. Where the house (a 'gallery flat' they called it) was to be was just a hole in the roof, full of dusty beams.

Two years later, I moved to Montrose Street, up in the roof again, in Miller Homes' converted warehouse where shirts and skirts and slacks had once been stitched on piece-rates. From my window, I can see Cochrane Street becoming St Vincent Street and stretching West into the sunset. It is the best view in Glasgow. The dome of the City Chambers, illuminated in the winter months, shines silver against fiery clouds and navy blue skies.

I am at home. This is my village. My corner shop is Marks and Spencers. My front garden is George Square, replete with French marigolds, geraniums, begonias, depending on the seasons. My neighbourhood pub is Babbity Bowsters, full of other Merchant City incomers, young hairdressers, old artists, the occasional actor, teachers, journalists ('bunch of bloody posers' as I have heard them called, slightly unfairly) but also genteel ladies in hats taking tea with gateaux, unemployed youngsters making lager last a long time.

My neighbourhood pub is Babbity Bowsters, full of other Merchant City incomers, young hairdressers, old artists, the occasional actor, teachers, journalists . . .

'I can swallow up great gulps of Glasgow's culture and there's always the entertainment free outside the door.'

It's all very nice, but we do ask ourselves sometimes, is it a betrayal of our roots? 'Do any real people live there?' a young man from Dennistoun asked me once, disparagingly. 'I'm a real person' I whined. But am I? Is it REAL to live in sophisticated little studios, gallery flats, penthouses even, when families on low incomes live long bus-rides away, in housing schemes where a Marks & Spencer chicken cordon bleu would obliterate a large chunk of the dole money?

Dave MacLennan, talented artistic director of the Wildcat Theatre Company (*The Steamie, Celtic Story, Border Warfare*) couldn't handle it. 'I feel guilty', he told me. 'I feel this part of Glasgow should have been regenerated to provide economical-rent housing for Glaswegians whose grannies were born nearby.' He moved west.

But the stark truth is, it could only happen this way. The centre of a city is important, whether it's Venice or Berlin, Manchester or Montreal. It needs shops and restaurants and offices and banks, but it also needs people. Otherwise it dies every night, the way Glasgow used to do, silent unlit streets no one would want to tread.

Fraser Laurie is mein over-the-top host of Babbity Bowsters, the nearest thing to an old coaching inn you'll find in Glasgow. With the beard and the eye patch, he's used to everyone saying he looks like a pirate, but really he's a philosopher and pundit, like his brother Tom, a driving force in inner city design, folk music and art.

There's *Glasgow Herald* arts buff John Fowler, tucked in a trendy garret ten seconds from his office; a beehive of Vidal Sassoon hairdressers from Princes Square; a smattering of students; a conglomeration of computer bores; a few rag traders; and lots of vaguely interesting-looking people who never let on what they do for a living but manage to afford oysters in Rab Ha's, suits in Ichi Ni San's and innumerable parking tickets. And, truly, a whole bunch of real people struggling to pay their mortgages, living on rice and with no furniture, because they reckon it's worth forking out every bit of disposable income to be in a place like this.

They all, often, bump into each other, at the theatre, at the beautiful Print Studio gallery, in the pub, at the Folk Festival or the Jazz Festival, or Mayfest. There is a lot going on, as the logo says especially in the glorious year of 1990.

I don't think I could have done a fraction of it if my kick-off point hadn't been here in the heart. From my flat, I can swallow up great gulps of Glasgow's culture within walking distance. I can trot to the Tron, stroll to the Royal Scottish Academy of Music and Drama or the Theatre Royal, shuffle along to the Kings or the Mitchell, hike up to the Third Eye Centre, hitch a lift to the Glasgow Arts Centre, take a bus to the Cranhill Arts Centre, a taxi to the Scottish Ballet Studios, walk to the Citizens. →

e Family Group 1948-49

The Art of Making
More People Amicable

Scottish Amicable are pleased to be Prime Sponsors
of the Glasgow 1990 Cultural Capital of Europe celebrations.

SCOTTISH AMICABLE

Scottish Football League Centenary
1 JUN

One hundred years of Scottish Football – sometimes it seems like 10,000 years – are celebrated this year as Scotland makes its fifth attempt in succession (known locally as Fiveinaro) to bring home the World Cup. Should they succeed, another strand of Glasgow's culture will be celebrated – with a vengeance.
Good luck to the Tartan Army, 'The best behaved supporters in the land.' And to the Scottish League, who will be organizing a banquet, a major game, a book and a video to celebrate.

The Art of J D Fergusson
1 JUN TO 31 JUL
BARCLAY LENNIE FINE ART
THE FINE ART SOCIETY

A treat for lovers of Fergusson, arguably the Scottish Colourist with the best chance of immortality. For the first time ever there will be a full viewing of the J D Fergusson Foundation's collection. With watercolours and drawings at Barclay Lennie and oils at The Fine Art Society.

Mackintosh in Context
1 JUN TO 31 AUG
GLASGOW SCHOOL OF ART

Previous exhibitions about Mackintosh have tended to isolate the man and his work. This exhibition attempts to place Mackintosh in the context of other leading architects and designers of the period. After all, architects like Sir James Milner, Sir J J Burnett and William Leiper had a significant effect on Glasgow's cityscape. The exhibition reveals Mackintosh's awareness of other dominant architectural styles at the end of the nineteenth century.

00063

And there's always innate entertainment to be found free outside the door. Just along the road the splendid statue of Mercury (god, appropriately, of commerce) has just been erected elegantly on its plinth high on top of the Italian Centre in Cochrane Street. A wee wummin, as we call them in Glasgow, digs me in the ribs: 'Haw hen. They've left wan o' their workmen up there!' she cackles.

taking time to see

**Article by
John Gordon
Sinclair**

*Famous as Gregory
in Bill Forsyth's
Gregory's Girl; one
of Scotland's most
popular actors.*

*… if I stay away from the
city for too long, I get
withdrawal symptoms.*

JOHN GORDON SINCLAI

What is this life if full of care.
We have no time to stand and stare.

When William Henry Davies wrote these words he had obviously just visited the wonderful city of Glasgow.

My love affair with Glasgow started some seven or eight years ago when I moved away from it to live in London. It wasn't until I started to return there on an increasingly regular basis that I began to notice what an attractive city Glasgow is. I never realized it had so many trees or public parks. The air, even in town, smelled quite fresh, breathing didn't seem dangerous. On top of that it had some really wonderful buildings to look at.

It is very easy to get carried away and walk around looking up continuously. It's a good idea, however, to occasionally watch in front of you. Many's the bloodied nose, blackend eye or soiled shoe I've had as a result of banging into poles or walking into fellow pedestrians.

As with all great love affairs, absence has only served to make my heart grow fonder to the point where, if I stay away from the city for too long, I get withdrawal symptoms. My Scottish accent begins to fade, I have to stand in a shower with all my clothes on, sit in the fridge then pop myself into the oven at Gas Mark 3 for half an hour before I feel normal again. In recent years, I have seen the face of Glasgow change quite considerably, mostly for the better. Glasgow has managed to retain some of the finest examples of Victorian architecture in Europe (possibly even the world). Instead of making way for the new, they now clean up and improve the old.

A stroll down West Nile Street, or my favourite, St Vincent Street, towards George Square, ending up at the magnificent City Chambers – best appreciated at night – will confirm this point of view. Whole sections of the city were built for the visit of Queen Victoria in 1888. The whole of Glasgow was given a facelift so that Glasgow would appear much more opulent than it was!

From Park Crescent, looking down through the park, you can see the resplendent red sandstone of the Art Gallery. It's said that the architect of this building, upon hearing that the intended route of the main road was to be diverted around the back of the gallery by the city planners, was so offended because the people passing in their carriages would not see the front of his work but the rear – climbed to the top of one of its towers and jumped off. Just to the right of the gallery, you see the baroque spires of Glasgow University jutting into the sky. It is one of the oldest universities in Britain, though every town I have ever visited claims the same for their university. Blackened by years of city grime, which oddly enough compliments the buildings, the University is an impressive sight, well worth a visit.

No mention of Glasgow and architecture would be complete without the name Rennie Mackintosh cropping up. He alone is responsible for what has been nicknamed 'the Glasgow Style'. His influence has never been more strong than it is today. The beautiful Princes Square, just off Buchanan Street, is a modern shopping mall which was designed by George McKith and Hugh Martin and Partners with an obvious Mackintosh feel. The Glasgow School of Art in Renfrew Street and the *Herald* building in Albion Street are just a couple of examples of his brilliant work that can still be seen today. In the past Glasgow has been better known for its more infamous activities. Its great to be given the opportunity that 1990 will provide to show off the positive side of Glasgow, a side that has always been there but simply overshadowed. See for yourself!

THERE'S
A LOT
GLASGOWING
ON IN
1990.
CULTURAL CAPITAL OF
EUROPE

1 9 GO 9 0

GLASGOW

Peel off

PROUD TO BE PART OF GLASGOW IN 1990.

JUNE

The Big Day

2 TO 3 JUN
CITYWIDE

Glasgow's huge summer street spectacle. A Green party with a difference. Over the weekend of 2/3 June, Scotland's top bands and rock attractions go open air on Glasgow Green in a *free* concert to celebrate the cultural year.

In George Square and surrounding city-centre streets, there will be non-stop music on several stages, entertainment, busking, food, street theatre and performance. Reckoned to be the largest street party the world has ever seen, the entire event will be televised live. A day to keep free in the diary, a day to leave the car at home . . .

The Art Machine

2 JUN TO 26 AUG
McLELLAN GALLERIES

Good fun with a serious purpose in one of the most exciting exhibitions in the calendar: the largest ever mounted in Britain exclusively for – and mostly by – children and young people. Through workshops, exhibitions, displays or just talking, the aim is to give children and young people a hands-on experience of the materials and processes of creation and to give adults a greater awareness of art and design.

Cities for the 21st Century

2 TO 10 JUN
SCOTTISH EXHIBITION & CONFERENCE CENTRE/ FORUM HOTEL

Cities for the 21st Century is an international exhibition and conference devoted to the future of post-industrial cities. It will examine what roles can be played by new technologies, global transportation and telecommunications in shaping these futures.

times past

**Article by
Jack House**

*Author of numerous
books, including
Down the Clyde.*

'One day in London
when Adam Smith
was boasting of
Glasgow, Johnson
turned to him with a
withering look and
said, "Pray sir, have
you ever seen
Brentford?"
However, when
visiting Glasgow in
1773, and being
shown the
Cathedral, Boswell
asked if he felt
"some remorse" —
for perhaps the only
recorded moment
in Johnson's
lifetime he was
silent.' **(Literary
Landmarks of
Glasgow – James
A. Kilpatrick, 1898)**

J A C K   H O U S E

**How did St Mungo get to Glasgow? This is where you will
have to start working on your Suspension of Disbelief.**

His mother was a saint. Her name was Thenew and there was a
St Thenew's chapel in Glasgow at one time. Glaswegians are very fond of
corrupting names and somehow or other St Thenew became St Enoch.
Princess Thenew was very beautiful and a Christian when Christianity
was just beginning to come to Scotland. She was the daughter of King
Loth of Lothian, who was no Christian.

Young neighbouring nobleman, Prince Ewen, dressed himself as a girl and
arrived late one night. He sought out the Princess and asked to share her
bed. She willingly agreed and trustingly welcomed him into her arms. The
Princess had vowed to be a virgin and couldn't understand why she was
putting on weight. When her father discovered what had happened he
was as wroth as ever a Loth could be. He ordered that his daughter be
taken to the Bass Rock in the Firth of Forth and be thrown over the highest
cliff that could be found.

But the King's retainers were taken aback when, just as the Princess
hurtled from the top of the cliff, a flight of white birds appeared. They flew
below and round her and carried Thenew to the North Berwick shore
where a convenient coracle awaited. The birds guided the Princess into it
and, of its own volition, the coracle pushed itself out and sailed across to
the opposite shore, landing at the holy place of Culross.

At Culross there was a monastery and also a school for boys run by
St Serf. Soon after she went ashore Thenew's baby was born and it was a
son. Such an event can't have taken place since another noble lady found
Moses in the bulrushes. St Serf not only tended the Princess but also
decided to bring up the boy. He named him Kentigern, which meant 'noble
lord' in the Highland language, and Mungo, meaning 'dear one' in the
Lowland tongue.

Mungo was not popular at school. St Serf doted upon him and the other
pupils decided that he was the 'teacher's pet'. They did their best to get
him into trouble. It was a rule at the monastery that each boy had to take it
in turn to sit by the fire all night to make sure it wouldn't go out. By some
trick they managed to get Mungo sound asleep. When he did wake up, he
found that the fire he was supposed to tend was black out. →

JUNE

It's fitting that Glasgow has been chosen to host this major event. It is widely appreciated that the city has led the field in both urban renewal and in dealing with the long-term task of encouraging the industries of the future.

The World Highland Games Championships

9 TO 10 JUN
CARMUNNOCK

Another sporting first for 1990. Athletes will come from the USA, Canada, Australia and New Zealand to confront the home talent.

The quality of competition is likely to better anything in the history of traditional Highland Games.

There will be the customary tests of strength and technique in Hammer Throwing, Putting the Stone, Tossing the Caber, lifting the McGlashan Stones and throwing the 28lb and 56lb weights.

The Games will be accompanied by International Piping and Dancing competitions. Massed Pipe Bands will play traditional music, and both Scottish Country dancers and Scottish Highland dancers will show their skills.

Glasgow Heritage Week

9 TO 17 JUN
CITYWIDE

The National Trust for Scotland was formed in the early 1930s. This month the Trust presents the fifth **Glasgow Heritage Week**. The programme is designed to raise public awareness of over 6,000 years of local history. A range of guided walks, heritage trails, bus tours, slide talks, lectures and exhibitions will offer broad access to the city's heritage.

'(Sheriff) Alison lives in style, in a handsome country house out of Glasgow, and is a capital fellow, with an agreeable wife, nice little daughter, cheerful niece, all things pleasant in his household. I went over the prison and lunatic asylum with him yesterday (December 29); at the Lord Provost's had gorgeous State lunch with the Town Council; and was entertained at a great dinner-party at night. Unbounded hospitality and enthoozymoozy the order of the day, and I have never been more heartily received anywhere, or enjoyed myself more completely.'

(Charles Dickens in a letter to John Forster, 1847)

That didn't worry St Mungo at all. He went over the frostbound ground and pulled a bough from one of the leafless trees. He brought the bough into the monastery, put it down in the fireplace and commanded it to burst into flames, which it promptly did.

When St Mungo grew up he decided to leave his unpopularity behind him. Like a wise man of the East he decided to go West. He said his farewells to the ageing St Serf, who told him of a lodging along the way where a holy man named Fergus would take him in for the night. So Mungo faced the setting sun and trudged along what passed for a highway in those days and eventually reached the home of Fergus.

He found Fergus on his death-bed. He tried to look after the dying man, who knew he would not last the night. Fergus whispered a last wish to Mungo, asking him to see to his burial. He said there was a cart outside and his body was to be placed on it and the cart drawn by two untamed bulls. Mungo was not to drive the bulls. He was to follow them and where they stopped Fergus was to be buried. Mungo went out and found a cart near by, but there was no sign of any bulls. He went back to Fergus and did his best to comfort him in his dying moments.

The next morning he went out soon after dawn and there he saw two wild bulls. They proved easily manageable and Mungo had no difficulty in harnessing them to the cart. As soon as he placed the body of Fergus on the cart, the bulls started for the West with St Mungo following them. They travelled some thirty miles before they stopped in a pleasant glen, facing a great grey rock with a beautiful burn purling between just below St Mungo's vantage point.

He liked the look of this place so much that he decided to build his cell here, and establish a religious community if he could. The Molendinar was the beautiful burn at the foot of the glen. The great grey rock was later named the Fir Park and became the necropolis of the Merchants' House of Glasgow. St Mungo set up a monastery where Glasgow Cathedral stands today and this is generally accepted as the birth of Glasgow. The date was AD543.

looking back

Article by

Jeremy Isaacs

Founding chief executive of Channel 4; now General Director of the Royal Opera House.

JEREMY ISAACS

Glasgow, for most of those of us growing up in it in the 1940s, was the only city of culture we knew. It cared then, as it cares now, about books and music, and theatre and paintings.

The city was famed for the Orpheus Choir, which I never cared for, but after the wireless and a few scratchy 78s – Chabrier's 'Espana' and Amelia Galli-Curci singing 'Lo Hear the Gentle Lark', and much sharpening of horn needles and winding the gramophone — my musical education took off in subscription concerts to the Scottish Orchestra in St Andrew's Hall on Saturday nights, and, before that, on Sunday afternoons at Green's Playhouse.

Green's Playhouse was supposed to be the cinema with the largest capacity in Europe, 8,000. We sat in the golden divans. My mother

drove us in her little grey Vauxhall, CWP 617. I heard J. Wright Henderson play Beethoven's First Piano Concerto and saw, I write the word advisedly, Thomas Beecham conduct. For the Polonaise from *Eugen Onegin* he came off his rostrum, cleared a space and danced in front of the strings. Beecham conducted a sort of teasing quarrel with the Glasgow audience. By message to the *Glasgow Herald* in advance he warned us, if we had coughs and colds, to stay away from his concerts, and not to spoil them by noisy hacking and spluttering as we had, according to him, in the previous year. And at Green's Playhouse, before an encore, the orchestra manager announced that Sir Thomas challenged the distinguished Glasgow audience 'to recognize this familiar masterpiece'. It was sometimes hard, after a lavish Sunday lunch – Scotch broth, roast beef, Eve's pudding – to →

Alison Johnson

'Saint Mungo, patron saint of Glasgow, founded the "High Church of Glasgow" in 632, although building did not start until 1077, by John Achaies, Bishop of Glasgow. The story of the fish and the ring comes from St Mungo's time. An "honest woman" lost her wedding ring and pleaded for St Mungo's help in order to pacify her husband who thought she was being unfaithful. St Mungo commanded the fisherman to bring him the first fish caught — this was duly brought to him and inside the fish's mouth the ring was found.' (**The History of Glasgow — John McUre, 1830**)

keep awake in the golden divans, but not for Beecham, and not for the big tunes of the Tchaikovsky symphonies, particularly the beginning of the last movement in the Fourth. That would wake anyone up.

The great pianists all came to St Andrew's Hall for the Saturday night series, Arrau, Moisewitch, Magaloff, Edwin Fischer, Malcuzynski (he broke a string in Rachmaninov's Third). But I remember best Kathleen Ferrier in Gerontius and Purcell, and a magical evening when Peter Pears and Dennis Brain joined the orchestra for Mozart – Horn Concerto No. Four and the tenor arias from *Don Giovanni* – and Britten. The orchestra under Walter Susskind gave the 'Grimes Sea Interludes'; Brain and Pears gave

us the Serenade for tenor, horn and strings. I can hear it all.

Susskind had his critics (they said he was no orchestra trainer), but I owe him a lot. I remember the silence that followed his conducting of Mahler's Ninth, at a time when Mahler was played rarely, and I remember the première in Glasgow of the Vaughan Williams Sixth. The woman in front of me observed to her neighbour at the start of the evening: 'It would be quite a good concert tonight, if it wasn't for this new piece by this… this, eh… Vaughan Williams.' But the new symphony was an instant hit, winning the poll to be heard again at the request concert at the end of the season.

For film, there was the Cosmo in Rose Street, and in the Gorbals, wedged in the then still standing stone-built street, the old Princess theatre, the Citizens. It always seemed to me to be full when we were there to see the plays of James Bridie or Paul Vincent Carroll, but what I remember best is the laughter at a pantomime that Bridie helped write, *The Tintock Cup*; it ran till Easter, with a laugh every thirty seconds. There had, by tradition, to be thirteen letters in the name of a panto at the Princess; *The Tintock Cup* had the right number. It also had both Duncan Macrae and Stanley Baxter as the dames in one scene, 'hinging oot the windaes' and, in another, in the powder-room of the Palais, 'Here Bella! Take my partner. I'm sweating.' First Macrae, then Baxter a year later, were lured away by Howard & Wyndhams to play elsewhere in the city at the Alhambra or the King's.

On winter mornings in January and February 1946 a long queue snaked its way in the snow round the City Art Gallery in Kelvingrove. The exhibition was of Picasso and Matisse – the work they had done in occupied France during the war, and, a little, if I remember, after it. The pictures in their strange forms and bold colours made a strong impact on me, and have not yet lost their power to do so. I soon discovered the treasures of the Gallery, the great Rembrandt Young Man in Armour and the Bernard Van Orly Madonna, and the Pre-Raphaelites – a bit chocolate-boxy these – and the wonderful Cézanne and the Manets and the Degas and the Sisley that belonged to the Burrell and are now housed separately there.

JUNE

SNO Proms

15 TO 30 JUN
KELVIN HALL

The **Scottish National Orchestra Proms** push the boat out for 1990. The twelve concerts once again combine the traditional with less well-known names and sounds. And, as ever, the emphasis will be on music and fun. One concert features a programme of Gilbert and Sullivan (19 June), conducted by Sir Peter Maxwell Davies! Carl Davis conducts a night of film music (20 June). Norman del Mar conducts Beethoven's **Choral Symphony**. The Choir of King's College, Cambridge makes its Scottish debut in a programme of Haydn and Fauré (21 June), before opening the **Chorus International Festival**.

The Irish Feis

16 JUN TO 1 JUL

The Irish Feis last year was attended, sponsored and supported by a variety of people from An Comhdhail to the Gaelic Athletic Association and was a riproaring success. This year's promises to be even better. So if you are Irish (or American, Scottish, Japanese or English) come into the parlour!

Chorus International

22 TO 29 JUN
THE ART GALLERY AND MUSEUM, KELVINGROVE

This two week festival of choral music further extends Glasgow's musical calendar for 1990. Some of the finest professional choirs and ensembles in Europe will be taking part. And audiences will be able to hear some of the most innovative music for voice ever written. The season also includes workshops and talks.

The Choir of King's College, Cambridge opens the festival performing music by →

Image by
Victoria Cassidy

'Like most artists, I work twice as hard, twice as long, for half the reward, and call it pleasure.'

the spirit of the city – a meditation

ROBIN McHAFFIE

Article by
Robin McHaffie

Minister of Kinning Park Parish Church, and Chairman of the Inter Church Committee for Glasgow 1990.

There is a great Spirit within us and a huge task ahead. The task is to weave love, peace and justice into the fabric of the new Glasgow.

Throughout 1990 we will celebrate the Spirit of the City; past, present and yet to come. As we 'backward glance' we know that we have much to learn from the past. The clash of diverse claims to truth, our loud heritage of schisms and the echoing of religious stances may not be pleasing music. To listen is to discover the cost in human terms of a growing culture.

As we survey our present the pride we feel in the physical renewal of Glasgow needs to be matched with a humility before the Spirit who seeks another renewal. We need to ask if the themes of justice, fellowship and universal love are being woven into the fabric of a new city.

To visualize our future in humility might be even harder. Yet I believe humility is the key which will unlock the city gate and let the Spirit of renewal work and grow. Keep that gate locked and our children will be trapped by the same cultural baggage, dogmas and injustices that weigh us down. We owe our kids the right to walk with the Spirit of the City hand in hand into their future.

We are

Perhaps you have watched children learning to walk? They stand holding on to the furniture when you know that inside them is an instinct pressing them to let go and step boldly into the middle of the floor. There is a parallel with many adult Glaswegians today. We watch this remarkable physical renewal around us. We are confronted with changing cultural patterns. We freeze and become white knuckled holding on to our own familiar furniture. We will not let go and follow our instincts. We are afraid of entering a spiritual renewal of our city.

confronted

If we believe in real progress we have no choice but to let go and walk. Of course we will bump into things, fall over and clash with the other toddlers learning to walk the same paths. That is the reality of the learning process.

with changing

As a committed Christian I see no choice but to let go. As a Christian society we have the true claims of Christ beside us and a Kingdom ahead. We are pilgrims together seeking the right path to our common future. →

cultural

patterns.

We are pilgrims together seeking the right path to our common future.

One of my early learning difficulties on this spiritual journey was in coming to terms with the clash of two statements by Jesus. The first, 'Blessed are the peacemakers', and the second, 'Do you think I came to bring peace on earth? No, I tell you, but division.'

This contrast alarmed me. I found a way through in the rhythms of life around us. The dualism of nature is quite apparent. It can be 'red in tooth and claw' as Blake describes it in *The Tyger*. It can be as peaceful as the cat washing herself on my daughter's knee. This essential dualism seems to be woven into the Creator's handiwork and the history of His errant children.

I now clearly perceive it in Christ with the Gospel that heals and the Gospel that bites. The people of Israel know it well. In his pastoral letter to the exiles in Babylon, Jeremiah counsels the people to settle and to seek the peace and prosperity of the city. A little later we read, '. . . all your enemies will go into exile. Those who plunder you will be plundered.' From such as this I learned that a ministry has to be both healing and confrontational if we are to guide the pilgrims through this journey.

be a hunter/gatherer on these banks. The earth would yield reluctantly and the winters were long. Yet the Celts stopped and meditated. Behind the ambivalence of all the forces they saw God and let God be God. Celtic writing has a mystic serenity that seems to arise from meeting at the dualism of creation and reflecting on the rhythms of life.

The peace we seek for our children will not come if we ignore any potentially-conflicting forces within a city.

The peace we seek for our children will not come if we ignore any potentially-conflicting forces within a city. Nor will it come if we abandon the struggle with the deep issues of peace and justice within the economic and other divisions of the city. Without peace, truth and justice our culture is dead. Touched by the 'spirit' of renewal it will live with hope in its soul.

Having part of the Clyde in my parish provides a powerful image. The timelessness of its rhythmic flow reminds me that part of who we are comes from the mists of our Celtic past. Our ancestors let God do things. That is not something that even the churches are very good at today. As I watch all the new buildings rising on the banks of our river I wonder if we are crowding God out by our bustle and our preoccupation with the renewal of 'things'.

My ancestors standing here had to struggle with the moods of Creation. It must have been hard to

From Calcutta a modern mystic offers a word to all cities. To all the inevitable 'why' questions arising from the poverty and misery of untimely death Mother Theresa will answer, 'It is God's will.' Her serenity and trust have emerged from harsh realities and profound divisions. Asked about her personal history, she once said, 'It is not important now. The important thing is to follow God's way and do something beautiful for Him.' This is the 'Spirit of the City'. This is the universal love that will heal and bring peace if allowed the freedom to enter our city gate. As we move to celebrate Glasgow in 1990 we can make space for this Spirit. If we can keep faith with this task then our festival may touch depth, meaning, hope and vision. Herein lies our growth.

Here is a prayer, after St Patrick, for 1990:

At Glasgow within this year of celebration

We place our sky with all its moods

our land with all its possibility

our river with its new found life

our labour with all its industry

our leisure with all its gaiety

our service the one to the other

our art with all its searching

our people with all our diversity

our future with all our hopes

All this and more we place

Before the spirit of the city.

JUNE

Herbert Howells, and Duraflé's Requiem, as well as the première of a commissioned piece by Martin Dalby (22 June). Other participating groups include: Vocem (25 June), La Groupe Vocale de France (23 June), The Collegium Vocale from Ghent (26 June) and the Hilliard Ensemble from England (28-29 June). Cappella Nova complete the festival with performances of all five masses by Scotland's Renaissance genius, Robert Carver (30 June-8 July).

Glasgow International Jazz Festival

29 JUN TO 8 JUL
CITYWIDE

Every year, the **Glasgow International Jazz Festival** presents some of the finest artists and bands in the world. To celebrate 1990, the Festival mounts a special programme featuring some of the top performers and ensembles in European jazz. Expect the best this year. Also continuing is the Festival's successful programme of educational and workshop activities – including guest artists as composers in residence.

Cappella Nova Carver

30 JUN TO 8 JUL
GLASGOW CATHEDRAL

Robert Carver was a Renaissance choral genius. Born in Scotland around 1490, he composed masses and motets for services at the Chapel Royal, Stirling. In 1990, 500 years after his birth, Cappella Nova performs his complete masses in a five concert series at Glasgow Cathedral. This, it's believed, is the first time all five masses have been performed together.

rab c. nesbitt's glasgow fair eight hundred

IAN PATTISON

Article by
Ian Pattison

*Has written for
Naked Video, Kick
up the Eighties and
Spitting Image.*

Whut? Eight hunner year of the Glesga Fair? Aye, well keep trying, we might get a dry one yet. Christ, don't talk to me about the Fair. I've got memories, boy, memories!

I still bear the emotional scars of being transported annually for a fortnight's penal servitude to Rothesay. Christ what a place thon is, Rothesay. It's got a faster inflation rate than Argentina. As soon as the calendar says July the fourteenth up jook the prices twenty-five per cent! Holidays is it? Christ there's not enough sand on Rothesay beach to cover a good boak, let alone bury the wife and weans so yi can slope off for a fly pint. In fact, know the best thing yi can say about Rothesay? At least it isnae Dunoon. What a gaff that is, by the way. All the atmosphere of the interior of a wardrobe. Built for the nuclear age. Only toon in the hemisphere to have achieved total melt down of the human spirit. Even saying the name makes yi feel as if it's started drizzling on the roof of your mouth. Dun-oon!

Only toon in the hemisphere to have achieved total melt down of the human spirit.
Yi feel as if it's started drizzling on the roof of your mouth.

Looking back, oors was a typical Glesga family. Unhappy go lucky. Both my parents had jobs. My faither worked on the buses and my mother was a wumman. I had an older brother but he died in police custody. Every cloud has a silver lining though. When he croaked, I inherited his suit and trainers. But I must say it's pure gallus being asked to do a wee PR job for Glesga. Coz after all, Glasgow smiles better, in't it? Better than Calcutta anyway. But I'm allowed to slag the joint, I live here. Anyhow, all youse tourists, I hope yeez enjoy your visit to Scotland. Coz we're some people us, by the way, the Scots! Wha's like us, eh? Not many, thank Christ. Listen, yi couldnie lend me ten pence for a yuppie castle, could yi. . . ?

Image by
Kay Ritchie

*'Back to Glasgow
in time to enjoy
all that is
happening . . .'*

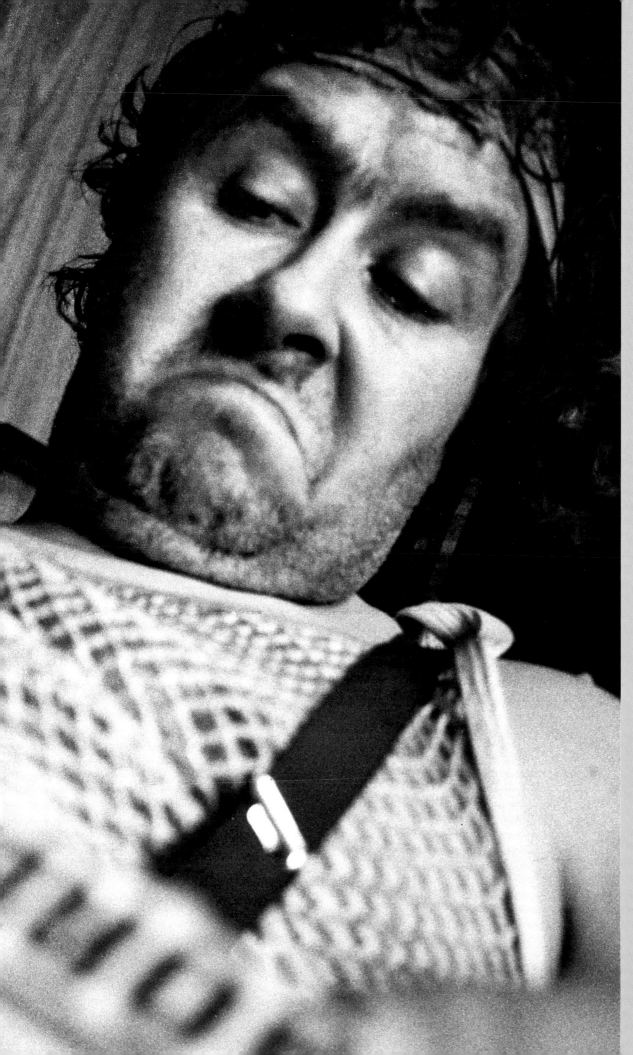

JULY

Aboriginal Arts

1 JUL TO 31 AUG
THIRD EYE CENTRE

The first exhibition ever seen in Glasgow of new art from Australia features new writing, rock bands, films, performances, workshops and children's events. This is the other side of Ramsay Street.

International Folk Festival

2 TO 8 JUL
CITYWIDE

The 1990 Festival will feature a full concert programme of the finest musicians and singers representing both traditional folk and world music. Folk dance ensembles from all over Europe and Scandinavia are coming to the Festival eager to encourage community participation. And the folk clubs and acts who do so much to keep the tradition alive will be given a well-earned high profile.

Les Liaisons Dangereuses

9 JUL TO 22 SEPT
THE MITCHELL THEATRE

First staged by the Royal Shakespeare Company at Stratford in September 1985 and currently in its fourth year at London's Ambassador's Theatre, it's now coming here. And for eleven weeks. This is the first time that a production, originated by the RSC has transferred to another British city whilst continuing to play in London on a commercial basis.

Hampton's adaptation of the Laclo's 1782 novel is set in the claustrophobic society of the eighteenth century French aristocracy. It portrays a world rife with sexual rivalry, riddled by intrigue and betrayal.

the artists

Article by

Tony Jones

Director, Glasgow School of Art 1980-1986; now President of the School of the Art Institute of Chicago.

TONY JONES

Throughout the world, it is increasingly the case that British trade now jets in behind the arts.

The painters, sculptors, muralists are part of a vanguard of expansion, a kind of cultural colonialism which threatens nobody and which can, if it is properly guided, bring huge benefits.

Many American cities have come to realize the importance of the arts in any comprehensive scheme of development and have set up a development plan for the arts and culture in relation to their own needs. Seattle is probably the most studied example of this approach.

From a very conscious platform, they have developed programmes for the arts and culture of their city which have resulted in Seattle establishing itself in the minds of Americans and foreigners as an attractive place to be. In many ways there are parallels between Seattle and Glasgow. They are both far removed from the centres of power and influence and both have suffered from a denigrating reputation: Glasgow as dirty and dangerous, Seattle as boring. Seattle has managed to turn that received opinion around and has become desirable. Glasgow is in the process of doing the same thing, but in an entirely different way.

Whereas in America the arts are being used by commerce and corporate industry in a conscious way, Glasgow has been successful by being completely informal. American cities are now beginning to look to Glasgow as an example of an integrated approach to culture.

Glasgow was boosted by the news that, as testament to the scale of regeneration, it has been awarded the title of Cultural Capital of Europe for 1990. The title first awarded to Athens in 1985 sets the city alongside Paris and Florence.

In that, history is repeating itself. There is a little-known letter written in 1902 by the Mayor of Chicago, Mayor Dunn, to the Lord Provost of Glasgow in which the Mayor boasts that 'Here in Chicago we are building the Glasgow of America'. It may seem unbelievable to many, but only ninety years ago Glasgow was in a position to send its city engineer to Chicago on loan to design and build the city's services.

In many other ways, Chicago is an echo of Glasgow. Where Glasgow has the Clyde as a living artery on the banks of which developed some of the most successful heavy industry in the world; so Chicago has Lake Michigan, by means of which it was able, like Glasgow, to become a major port. If the Clyde was one of the centres of shipbuilding, Chicago was the centre for meat processing and packing. The great Chicago poet, Carl Sandburg, describes Chicago as the 'hog butcher to the world'. →

Image by

Tommy

McMahon

'Glaswegians proud custodians of the gift of the gab.'

JULY

Eight Hundredth
Glasgow Fair

13 **JUL**
GLASGOW GREEN

For July 1990, and Glasgow Fair Fortnight a number of east end organizations have planned a spectacular re-enactment of the Glasgow Fair. After all, it's 800 years old this summer. Loud, brash and popular, this event combines the modern fun fair that comes every year to the Green with a Victorian Fun Fair. So ride on the Chair O' Planes and the hobby horses.

A Rerr Terr Arraferr

13 **JUL TO 21 DEC**
THE PEOPLE'S PALACE

This is an extensive exhibition, delineating 800 years of Glaswegians having a Rerr Terr (a Good Time) during the traditional two weeks of high jinks and haughmagandie (hanky-panky) in July. From the feeing fairs which were the origin of the Ferr to the trips 'Doon the Watter' – this should be a Rerr Terr.

The Italia Cup

14 **JUL**
NEWLANDS TENNIS CLUB

The Italia Cup, the over thirty-five men's international team event, is being brought to Glasgow this year by the International Tennis Federation. This will be the first ITF tournament ever to be staged in Scotland and around eighty players from twenty countries are expected, including John Lloyd, Nastase and Connors.

Scottish Art and Design,
3000 BC – 1990

14 **JUL TO 23 SEPT**
McLELLAN GALLERIES

Five thousand years of furniture, ceramics, glass, textiles, painting and sculpture with exhibits drawn from →

While both cities have lost a great deal of their traditional industry, the work which gave them an identity, they both have a resilience which enables them to adapt readily to changing circumstances.

In architecture there are other parallels. Just as Chicago had Louis Sullivan followed by Frank Lloyd Wright, Glasgow had Thomson followed by Mackintosh.

When I first came to Glasgow in 1970, there was a terrible sense, or rather an absence, of confidence. The environment was dull and bleak and there was a feeling of being in a backwater. The seeds of change were already in place, but it took until about 1980 for those seeds to begin to show above the ground. There were indications that something could develop in the arts which could be of wide significance. And this feeling was echoed in other areas of city life – in city government as much as in industry and commerce. But, again, the lead came from the artistic sector.

From 1981 the different streams of change became a tidal wave which has swept into existence the new Royal Scottish Academy of Music and Drama, the Scottish Exhibition and Conference Centre and several other developments. Vital people like Giles Havergal at the Citizens Theatre and the people at the Theatre Royal all contributed to the wave. And flowing alongside came those painters from the Glasgow School of Art who have now become established as the leaders of the New Figuration School. Steven Campbell is now in several major collections in America and several others, like Howson and Currie, are also being collected.

All of this makes the city a kind of magnet which attracts other developments. So we got Britoil and the Savings Bank and now those who have had their fill of places like London are becoming aware that Glasgow is an attractive and exciting place, where things happen.

For the future Glasgow must continue to charge that magnet. It must speak loudly about its greatness and it must revive those links with Europe which were so secure in the past. It must, once again, become a European city. And it is all very well for the banks and other commercial sectors to set up development initiatives. They are important, but there must be a backdrop and that backdrop can only be provided by the arts.

The kind of support provided by local authorities is also vital. Here Glasgow has benefited in the recent past through the actions of local authorities which have cleaned up the city and been very supportive of developments such as WASPS (who provide studios for artists) and the Print Studio. All these things serve to charge the magnet.

During 1990, Glasgow must capitalize on the status of being Cultural Capital by making sure that the magnet is permanently charged.

Of course, many of the now established Glasgow painters of the younger school are represented either in groups or one-man shows during the City's reign as Cultural Capital. Perhaps even more exciting is the proposed exhibition at the McLellan Galleries in January which will bring together examples from some of the most impressive young artists from other parts of Britain. The British Arts Show 1990 will illustrate what is best in contemporary art in this country. The bringing together of young artists from East and West in the Third Eye's Reorienting-Looking East promises to be another fascinating chapter in the developing links with the Eastern block and yet another reason for us to celebrate the growing international reputation of one of the best galleries in Britain.

There is a rather pleasing kind of balance in the fact that the McLellan Galleries is just down the hill from Rennie Mackintosh's masterpiece, the Glasgow School of Art, and it is right and proper that CRM should be the subject of a major retrospective.

On a recent return to Glasgow I sensed in that same building – the Glasgow School of Art – a great optimism. There was a confidence that what was being attempted would be given its proper place and would be respected.

1990 can only reinforce in the minds of both native Glaswegians and the world at large the knowledge of just how rich Glasgow is in culture.

the artists

DR JAMES MORRISON

I was painting up above Alexandra Parade near the Monkland Canal, near the spot that the Monkland motorway now occupies. At that time the tenements were being demolished as a preliminary to building the new motorway. There was a particularly fine tenement there, standing on its own, with two men on its roof dismantling it. Every now and then an enormous stone would come crashing down the side of the building from the roof level and further shatter the already broken up pavement down below.

At half past ten everyone around me stopped to have his 'piece'. When the two men from the top of my building came down to ground level, they were told by their mates, 'Hey Jimmy, he's pentin' your buildin'.' The two men came over and Jimmy said, 'Chris' Mac you're buildin' it up's fast's we'r pullin' it doon.'

I heard footsteps in the lane behind me and a boy's voice 'Hey mister.' I ignored it. 'Hey mister.' I continued to ignore it, wishing to get on with my work undisturbed. After several more attempts to attract my attention he said: 'Ma daddy says: dae ye tak milk and sugar?' 'Just neat, nothing in it at all', I said. He came back later with a mug of hot black tea and a large jammy bun. I said 'That's very kind, thank your Dad from me.' The boy said 'Ther' he is up a' the windae' and there indeed was his father wearing a singlet and giving me a wave.

An elderly man stopped. He said: 'Put in yur pictur no tae be sorry about the folk tha' lived in thae hooses. Ah've lived in that hoose ower ther fur sixty-two years an when a came here first Greenfield Street wis a decent workin' class street wi' clean closes an' sterrs. Then a the scruff go' in an they made i' like whit it is noo. See him ower ther, the one-arm bandit a ca' him. Aye nickin' the lead an' copper aff the auld hooses aye an' aff the new buildin' sites tae. He knows a've got ma eye oan 'm an' a'll get 'm some day.'

Another old gentleman came along: 'See a live in tha' row therr. Terrible so it is. Wan night a heard ma door openin' and a went oot tae the lobby, an here's a man wi' a mask ower's heid an' haudin' a crowbar. A managed tae grab the crowbar an wrestled wi'm but a cut a' ma hand. He went away. It turned oot that' thur wus a man in the factor's office givin' sperr keys tae thae hard men an they wur robbin' folks' hooses, lettin' themselves in like. Anyway ye wid see it in the paper.' 'No, I'm sorry', I said 'I never saw it.' 'Aw come oan ye musta seen it it wis oan the front page.' 'What paper was that?' I said. *'The Govan Press'.*

Extract taken from Dr James Morrison's book *Aff the Squerr*

JULY

Glasgow's Museums and Galleries and Scottish collections will be on display at the McLellan Galleries. This huge exhibition will, for the first time, place Scottish art and design in a European context.

The European Special Olympics

20 TO 27 JUL
CITY & REGION

The Special Olympics are an international movement. They aim to give people with special needs the chance to play a full part in everyday society through year-round sports training and competitions. For 1990 Strathclyde Regional Council has invited the games to come to Scotland for the first time. Tournaments include volleyball, swimming, gymnastics, athletics and soccer. And these competitive events are staged alongside demonstrations of skill in cycling, tennis and table tennis. People of remarkable sporting abilities and talents will take part. The games were first held in Dublin in 1985. They are soon likely to be established on the Olympic quadrennial cycle.

The Queen's Return

27 JUL
CONTAINER TERMINAL, GREENOCK

This month, the magnificent QE2 returns to the Clyde for the first time since her launch and trials in the estuary. The one day visit is being made to mark European Cultural Capital year.
The public will be able to see her berthed on the Clyde once more. The return of the great Cunard vessel is sure to prompt memories amongst many of the John Brown's workforce who built her. It is hoped that visits aboard can be arranged during her brief stay.

a city fit for people

A N D Y   M A C M I L L A N

Article by
Andy MacMillan
Professor of architecture and head of the Mackintosh School of Architecture at Glasgow University.

'Glasgow is the emporium of the West of Scotland, being for its commerce and riches, the second in the northern part of Great Britain. It is a large, stately, and well-built city, standing on a plain in a manner four-square, and the five principal streets are the fairest for breadth, and the finest built that I have ever seen in one city together.'
(Daniel Defoe, during his visit in 1727)

...the need for modern hygiene in the wake of horrific cholera epidemics.

Glasgow is Scottish in its stone, European in its urban pedigree, American in its grid iron plan. It has a unique integrity and identity among the cities of Britain.

Little of its medieval past remains, save its stark High Church or Cathedral (1190-1450), deprived of its towers by Victorian 'restorers' but possessed of a fine collection of traditional and contemporary stained glass and a truly exceptional lower church. And Provands Lordship (1470) in the High Street, the oldest house in Glasgow, which dates from the end of the medieval era.

Renaissance Glasgow is largely gone too. The Tolbooth Steeple of 1626 and the Lion and Unicorn stair of the University remain from Jacobean times, the staircase having been taken to Gilmorehill when the University moved there in mid-nineteenth century to make way for a railway station. Pollok House (1737) by William Adam, father of the famous brothers, graces the estate which also contains the recent Burrell Museum (1982) by Barry Gasson. St Andrew's Church (1739) by Allan Dreghorn possesses a fine portico and tower and stands now in a newly restored residential Georgian square.

There is rather more left of Georgian Glasgow. Carlton Terrace (1802), facing the river, with Robert Adam's fine Trades House (1791) (Glasgow Masons' Guild Charter goes back to the eleventh century) and the Virginia Street Tobacco Exchange (1819) are prime examples. Something of the period's quality can still be felt in Blythswood Square (1820) where, around 1900, Mackintosh inserted into one side an interesting but disruptive doorway for the Glasgow Ladies Art Club.

The greatest period of Glasgow's building was in Victoria's reign when the city expanded explosively to meet the needs of its burgeoning engineering and chemical industries.

Much of historic Glasgow disappeared at the same time as the city fathers responded simultaneously to these demands and to the need for modern hygiene in the wake of horrific cholera epidemics. The twisting streets and overcrowded slums of the old City were swept away with a 'modern' disregard for history. A water supply, sanitary provision, utilities and public transport system were put in place which made Glasgow, for a time, the finest modern city in Europe.

...the oldest house in Glasgow dates back from the end of the medieval era.

The Glasgow city centre today is largely the product of that time. Recent conservation policies have seen the retention and adaptation of many of the finer buildings of the period. The introduction of new buildings behind preserved façades, and the exploitation of warehouse premises for retail and residential use, displays an awareness of the quality of Victorian architecture while leaving the city centre reasonably intact.

Noteworthy new commercial building types were developed from the mid-nineteenth century onwards including some of the oldest known cast iron office buildings. Gardner's Warehouse (1855) by John Baird in Jamaica Street and John Honeyman's Ca d'Oro building (1872) in Union Street, recently restored (and extended) after a fire, are exceptionally fine specimens of this genre. Together with the Kibble Palace glasshouse (1863) in the Botanic Gardens, these are probably three of the finest cast iron buildings in the world.

The University (1866) by Gilbert Scott, which was the second largest building contract in the world at that time, occupies an unforgettable site on a hill overlooking the River Kelvin in the west end park (Kelvingrove). And J W Simpson's fine Kelvingrove Art Galleries (c 1886) along with the City Chambers in George Square, epitomize the intense civic pride of the era.

Glasgow is fortunate in possessing the works of two native architectural giants, each unique. 'Greek' Thomson (1817-75) interpreted the needs of Victorian industrial society within the terms of reference of traditional classical architecture adhering, as he thought, to the principle of Greek architecture. He developed the concept of what later came to be called the curtain wall in his great Victorian office and warehouse developments: Dunlop Street (1849); the Grecian Chambers (1865); the Egyptian Halls (1871). Effectively, in Holmwood House (1856) in Cathcart and the Double Villa (1859) in Langside, he also invented the Prairie house some thirty years before Frank Lloyd Wright in America, and his many tenement and terrace blocks brought the art of street architecture to a fine pitch.

Great Western Terrace (1869), often held to be his best, is less innovatory externally than his Moray Place Terrace (1859) or Oakbank Avenue (1857) and Hyndland Road (1871). All are well worth a visit by any who profess to delight in urbane as well as urban architecture.

Glasgow's greatest architectural figure, however, surely must be Charles Rennie Mackintosh, arguably the most significant architect in Europe at the turn of the century. His Hill House (1902) in Helensburgh and Windyhill (1900) at Kilmacolm are among the great houses of the twentieth century and significantly influenced the development of functional architecture in Europe.

The Glasgow School of Art (1897-1709) in Renfrew Street is still a working art school nearly a hundred years on, and is probably the only building of international standing in Scotland. It is certainly the only one to have led an architectural style, rather than followed it. It combines utility, convenience and delight in its origin, it was intended as a plain building. Its strength lies in its presence, which remains Scottish yet functional, a particular building yet archetype in its effect. But essential Glasgow is a totality; Victorian town planning at its practical and pragmatic best.

Virtually one building form, the tenement, provides a matrix in which architectural embellishment is used to signal and structure hierarchy and place. A large measure of the unity of the town derives from the employment of this single building type and the consistent use of stone and slate which imports a dignity to the most ordinary of buildings.

The high residential density generated by the ubiquitous use of the tenement engenders a wealth of public building to enrich and particularize the main streets. Glasgow's bustling vigour is a by-product of its pragmatic architectural form. Commercial acumen and community pride locate unique architectural compositions on important corners and gushets, effectively landmarking the city for its users and making Glasgow memorable in the process. →

Image by
Andrew Foley

'I feel it is crucial to preserve national and traditional culture.'

JULY

Keyboard Music

30 JUL TO 11 AUG
THE ART GALLERY AND MUSEUM, KELVINGROVE/ PAISLEY ABBEY

At Kelvingrove, the Glasgow Harpsichord Society is staging three celebrity concerts, including one by Melvyn Tan. There will also be an exhibition of working historic and contemporary instruments. At the exhibition, during Museum opening hours, practical demonstrations will be given, and workshops in instrument construction will be held.
Later in the month, leading organists from all over the world will be in Strathclyde for the **Paisley International Organ Competition**. There will also be a series of recitals on the Paisley Abbey Cavaille-Coll organ, and on the recently restored Lewis organ in Kelvingrove.

Bolshoi Opera

31 JUL TO 5 AUG
SCOTTISH EXHIBITION & CONFERENCE CENTRE

The Bolshoi Opera from Moscow, one of the world's great opera companies, makes its first ever visit to the UK as part of Glasgow's 1990 celebrations.
The entire company of 450 singers and musicians are bringing their two classic productions of Mussorgsky's **Boris Godunov** and Borodin's **Prince Igor.**
And there will also be a new production of Tchaikovsky's **The Maid of Orleans** (text by Schiller). The Bolshoi's spectacular performances will feature the Soviet Union's finest soloists, the superstars of Russian opera.

FRANK A. WALKER

**Article by
Frank A. Walker**

*Architect and
author, teaching
architectural
history and design
at the University of
Strathclyde.*

By the end of the Victorian era the commercial-ization of Glasgow's First and Second New Towns, while not complete, was certainly assured. Warehousing dominated the streets of the old Merchant City. From Buchanan Street west to Hope Street high-rise office chambers rose from narrow residential plots, while many of the late-Georgian terraces still surviving on Blythswood Hill were no longer in domestic use. Now, a century later, the planning paradox of downtown Glasgow is the reversal of that trend, not simply in terms of the repopulation of the city centre but in the conversion of warehouse and office space to flatted accommodation and, latterly, in the construction of new infill housing. No lawyers or doctors or accountants have yet returned to take up house in Blythswood but, east of Buchanan Street, the residential recovery reaching as far as the Cathedral has effected a physical and social transformation.

The turn-about began around 1970 when students and staff at the architecture school in the University of Strathclyde began to explore the feasibility of saving the tenement, Glasgow's most ubiquitous and socially adaptable residential building type. Until then a *tabula rasa* policy of comprehensive redevelopment, pursued in the inner suburbs throughout the 1960s, had entailed the destruction of much of the city's ill-maintained but architecturally coherent tenemented townscape, clearing the ground for new housing districts of multi-storey towers. Glasgow's distinctive urban fabric, in which streets and houses were intimately related in humane four-storey scale, seemed to disappear altogether. Fortunately, the rot was stopped.

Michael Kuzmak

…pollution vanished in clouds of dust, a wealth of decorative detail was revealed in warm ochre or rust walls of sandstone.

First, clean air encouraged clean buildings and, as the black grime of a hundred and more years' pollution vanished in clouds of dust, a wealth of

decorative detail was revealed in warm ochre or rust walls of sandstone. Then, stimulated by grant aid, housing association direction, community participation and an economic recession, the programme of rehabilitation anticipated at Strathclyde gathered steam. Flats were refurbished, proper bathrooms and kitchens implanted, back courts were cleaned and greened: Partick, Maryhill, Springburn, Govanhill and Govan all began to recover.

*Warehousing and office
accommodation from the
1790s to the 1930s has been
turned into flats…*

By the start of the 1980s, the city administration was exploiting the possibilities of the housing market to produce a partnership of public and private investment, the strategy being to redeem the worst of the peripheral post-war housing estates and a blighted inner city. While the former task will continue to present a formidable challenge into the twenty-first century, the revitalization of the Merchant City, Glasgow's First New Town, is well advanced. City Improvement Trust tenements have been cleaned and renewed. Warehousing and office accommodation from the 1790s to the 1930s has been turned into flats (in at least one case, in Wilson Street, property built before the end of the eighteenth century as high grade flats but later adapted as warehousing, has been returned to its original use). New medium-rise infill housing, has healed the streetscape. Pubs, restaurants and shops have followed to provide the social cement. The formula is spreading. At Port Dundas a massive stretch of long-abandoned canalside warehousing, has been rehabilitated as flats. New riverside housing is appearing at Carrick Quay, Lancefield Quay and on the site reclaimed for the 1988 Garden Festival. Much of the market has been provided by a young affluent middle class, a social factor which, while it can produce quality work makes the need for a comparable solution for the city's less central housing areas all the more pressing.

What might this solution be? In some cases rehabilitation may still be the answer, whether this means tenement improvements or, more challenging, the saving of the outer suburbs. Important, too, are those cleared inner suburban areas adjacent to, and beyond, the Inner Ring motorway, particularly along its putative eastern and southern alignments. If these edges, once given over to housing, are to be won back to the same land use, bringing a better social balance to inner city living, an architectural answer, appropriately robust and flexible, will have to be found. The search need not be a protracted one, however, for no building type seems better fitted to the challenge than the Glasgow tenement itself.

Michael Kuzmak

. . . the tenement is an enduring model for inner city living.

Michael Kuzmak

The very need to insert infill housing beside rehabilitated tenements – a frequent design problem where, as in the Merchant City, Garnethill, Maryhill and elsewhere, the continuity of the streetscape demands it – has highlighted the problems in such a prescription. Architectural detail, materials and floor-to-floor heights are not those of Victorian times and attempts to marry the new to the old are often insubstantial and out of scale. Still, the case for the tenement is a compelling one – a standardized yet variable residential building form, it 'possesses the advantage in points of economy, in durability, in substantial appearance, in warmth and capacity for standing wear and tear . . .'. These arguments, first presented by a working-class committee in 1858, might today be augmented by a jargon of concern about townscape, energy conservation, micro-climate, social mix and defensible space but the case would still be sound: the tenement is an enduring model for inner city living.

In 1989 the competition-winning 'Tenement for the 21st Century' was built on Shakespeare Street, Maryhill. For the first time, by virtue of a four floor/six floor cross-section, new flatted architecture successfully matched the grain of the existing tenemented streets. Here at last was a pattern for the future.

Michael Kuzmak

helping hands

Article by
Colin Williams
*Director of Glasgow
Council for
Voluntary Service,
Chairman of
Goodwill, Secretary
to the Glasgow
Access Panel.*

COLIN WILLIAMS

For too many years people with disability have been patronized and discouraged from playing their full part in the life of the community. Out of sight and out of mind reflects the policies which led to the development of huge institutions located in the country and containing many who could live in the community.

The physical environment is hostile to anyone in a wheelchair or anyone with problems of blindness or deafness. Access to public services, buildings and to places of entertainment are generally no-go areas for anyone who has mobility problems. Wheelchairs cannot climb steps.

Both the Region and District have recently supported new initiatives to stimulate involvement in the creative arts by funding organizations. They have also contributed to the preparation of an access guide in preparation for the year of culture.

As part of Glasgow 1990, Strathclyde will host the European Special Olympics in July of the same year which will bring to the city over 3,000 competitors who experience problems of mental handicap. This reflects a commitment to supporting events which highlight the skills and strengths of individuals rather than focusing on their 'disability'. The games will offer practical experience on the logistics of quality provision for so many people with disabilities. Public, private and voluntary organizations, together with hundreds of volunteers are being brought together to manage this remarkable event. The lessons will be far reaching and should provide a solid foundation upon which services for the local population could be developed.

...a solid foundation upon which services for the local population could be developed.

Image by
Heather Nevay
'I love living in Glasgow'.

AUGUST

event. The art of flying will be demonstrated by many famous local, national and international flyers. Height of flight competitions will thrill the onlooker. And flocks of stunt kites will take to the air.

An attempt will be made on the world record for the number of kites in the air at the same time. The record is 500 kites flying simultaneously — set at the Washington Kite Festival. But records are there to be broken.

Glasgow Early Music Festival

4 TO 11 AUG
ROYAL SCOTTISH ACADEMY OF MUSIC & DRAMA/TRAMWAY

A compact but rich week of music making — some of it on the streets. That's the **Glasgow International Early Music Festival,** one of the musical highlights of 1990.

The city hosts some of the finest and most accomplished early music ensembles and artists in the world.

The most ambitious undertaking is the modern world première of Marazzoli's opera, **La Vita Humana** — it was last performed in 1656. Co-produced by the Scottish Early Music Consort and the Musikhogskolan i Malmö, Sweden, it is scheduled for two performances at Tramway. The piece will be directed by Warwick Edwards, produced by Kate Brown, choreographed by Andrea Francalanci with members of his Florence ensemble, Il Ballerino. Other world names include: La Grande Ecurie et la Chambre du Roy, directed by Jean Claude Malgoire; Tallinn's Hortus Musicus, director Andres Mustonen; and Melvyn Tan.

Quincities

4 AUG TO 3 OCT
90s GALLERY

The international quality of Glasgow is reflected in its connections with other cities. In this exhibition are gathered →

up the people

Article by
Tom McGrath

Playwright and Director, plays performed by the Traverse Theatre and the Royal Shakespere Company.

'No man can owe greater obligations to a society than I do to the University of Glasgow.' **(Adam Smith on his election as Lord Rector, 1787)**

...who's going to do the counting? They'll get cricks in their necks.

TOM McGRATH

Fancy flying a kite or making a magic lantern? Think about it for a moment. Maybe you've already said yes, but, on the other hand, there might be a disgruntled part of you that thinks you might have something better to do with your time. Or maybe you think the arts are irrelevant in view of the social problems that are all around. As one wee man in a bunnet put it, 'European City of Culture! Forget it! Pit some toilets in Queens Park then you cin tawk aboot effin culture.'

It's amazing nowadays what people expect the arts to be able to do. There has to be a limit. The arts can't build new houses but they can do other things. Maybe flying a kite is exactly what that wee man needs.

Even watching a kite fly can have its advantages, as Tibetans have long since known, and the people of Glasgow will get to try for themselves when a major Kite Festival floats into the blue of early August 1990.

Not only will people be able to watch kites fly, and see fabulous kite creations from all over the world, up in the sky and down on the ground, but they can learn how to make kites too. Likely Saint Mungo will trail his robes through the clouds, or the bird, the fish, the bell and the tree will suddenly learn to fly, because there is also going to be a competition for the best kite design on the theme of Glesca Culture. Watch out for the Birling Burrell. Charles Rennie Mackintosh takes to the sky. On one particular day the Glasgow skyline will get very crowded as who knows how many kite-fliers try to beat the world record for the number of kites flown in the sky at one and the same time. Who's going to do the counting? They'll get cricks in their necks.

Meantime, back on earth, out in the streets to be exact, StreetBiz will be amazing shoppers with street performances the likes of which they've never seen, even in the streets of Glasgow, where there's a lot of performers going around. Previous StreetBiz presentations have included marching bands from New Orleans, steel bands from Trinidad, acrobats from Ghana and something suspicious called 'artistes de la rue' – from France, of course. Watch out for lingerie in your shopping. If you fancy your chances on the spoons and tin whistle, robotic walking or Bob Dylan strums, then get your name down for the busking competition. You've got until August to get your act together. →

Image by
Calum Colvin

'It's the people who are the most important element in the identity of the city.'

AUGUST

StreetBiz

11 TO 26 AUG
CITY & REGION

For those who don't want to go to theatres for theatre — it's on the streets where you shop. StreetBiz, Glasgow's annual festival of street theatre, performance and entertainment takes place this month.

It's a truly international event. Marching bands from New Orleans, Trinidadian steel bands, acrobats from Ghana, leading artists de la rue from France, performers from India — these are just a few of the attractions from previous seasons.

Each year a special large-scale outdoor piece is commissioned as the climax to the event. Another annual highlight is the busking competition.

Glasgow's World Music Festival

31 AUG TO 2 SEPT
POLLOK PARK

The venue, Pollok Park, is one of Glasgow's most beautiful parks and enables the **World Music Festival** to be a multi-stage event. On view will be bands, solo musicians and a variety of performers in other media. Collaborative work between visiting musicians and players from communities in and around Glasgow will be a special feature. Some acts will also perform at other venues throughout the city. Apart from the music, there will be stalls selling a wide range of international crafts and food.

Oor Wullie's life is never borin'—

Here he is, awa' explorin'!

'And will it be able to flash like lightning?' asked the director, 'Yes,' said the stage manager. 'It will do all that.' It was director Gerry Mulgrew who heads the brilliant Scottish theatre company, Communicado. He was talking about a tramcar which Communicado was trying to hire for its production of *Jock Tamson's Bairns*, written by Glasgow poetess and dramatist supreme, Liz Lochhead, and described as 'more like a folk/jazz opera than a conventional play.'

It is the story of the Scottish people – where were they then, where are they going now – and it takes place at a surrealistic Burns Supper where all sorts of strange things start going on, apart from the haggis and scotch. It will be presented at the Tramway in February.

As well as presenting *Jock Tamson's Bairns*, Communicado will be offering workshops which are open to all. Contributors will include the amazing dancer Frank McConnell, the equally amazing artist, Keith MacIntyre and Liz Lochhead and Gerry Mulgrew. Also, during the run of the show, the technical and backstage Communicado workers will be giving conducted tours of the *Jock Tamson's Bairns* production to help people learn exactly how – in practical terms – a stageshow gets put on.

Will Gerry catch his tramcar? Whether he does or not, we can be sure that Communicado, who recently won the Prudential Insurance award for 'theatrical excellence' to the tune of £25,000, together with Liz Lochhead will come up with a show that will speak – and sing.

City is for everyone to be in. An embryonic version of it was performed at the Tramway in 1989, involving over 200 participants in what director Alan Lyddiard announced as only a small taste of what is to come. He's definitely a man for whom the whole world's a stage. In Dundee he took the audience round to see a play in double-decker buses, stopping at different scenes from the story along the way. In Glasgow he's planning to use the subway with scenes at every station. Lets hope the escalator's working. Then there's a canal – he's promising you a boat trip to experience the *City* action. And a galleon burning on the Clyde down near the boathouse at Glasgow Green. How long will the show last? Almost a year. But don't worry, the intervals last a month at a time.

The involvement of people with special needs has been a feature of *City* right from the outset, and the women who run Fablevision are adept at bringing the arts and people together. They ran a project in Kirklands Hospital, for example, which was performed by twenty mentally-handicapped residents along with some staff.

With Fablevision, people make magic theatre. Costume-maker and writer, Rita Winters, is a whiz with the velcro and you never know when watching their shows just when one of the costumes is going to suddenly transform itself and reveal another layer below.

Myth, mime, music and the female touch. Firmly rooted in the community, Fablevision makes theatre based on our imagination. Their *The Monster That Ate Barlanark* was a hit at the Mayfest. In the spring of 1990, they will launch a two-year community programme involving young, unemployed Glaswegians. This will culminate in what is known in theatre lingo as a 'promenade production'. Sounds very posh, doesn't it? What it means is that the audience gets to move about, and the performers to move among them. Lets go for a walk in the theatre. Promenade theatre is at least as old as the medieval sandal the archaeologists dug up in Glasgow recently, but it's the 1990 way.

Project Ability, which has been a driving force in the new movement to bring art and people with special needs together, has several major events in 1990 for people with disabilities.

The People's Palace is holding an exhibition about popular culture in Glasgow over 800 years. In July Glasgow Green will spring into life with a spectacular re-enactment of the Glasgow Fair. In October the Cranhill Arts Project will present Glaswegians by Glaswegians, a photographic exhibition, with Glasgow people showing their view of the place. Oh, yes, and also in January there's East End Banners at the People's Palace. There's going to be an Asian Bazaar in the Tramway. Oh, yes, and there's Jekyll and Hyde with Asian, Gaelic and Welsh people coming together. Which month is that happening? And the European Special Olympics. When is that? We're going to have to be handy with our diaries in 1990.

Glasgow people have always been pretty good at organizing things for themselves, one way or

If you fancy your chances on the spoons and tin whistle, robotic walking or Bob Dylan strums…

How long will the show last? Almost a year…

Promenade theatre is at least as old as the medieval sandal the archaeologists dug up in Glasgow recently…

An unprecedented social experiment is taking place…

another, and they are certainly rising to the 1990 occasion with several hundred neighbourhood events already in the making. Annual galas, festivals, community celebrations, and several hundred other projects are happening throughout Strathclyde in schools, community centres, adult training centres and art centres. Writing about it makes me feel breathless.

A massive effort is being made by everyone concerned – local and district authorities, community and educational workers, artists and art animators, arts councils, Mayfest, disability organizations, and, not least, the Glasgow people themselves. Whatever the cynics say, an unprecedented social experiment is taking place, with the arts and the community in the mix together, and support from every sector.

And what about those lanterns? There's going to be big ones and small ones, handheld and on the backs of trucks. Led by John Fox's Welfare State International and his Engineers of the Imagination, they want everyone to celebrate Glasgow as the City of Light. Wonder what the wee man will make of all that. Maybe he'll see the light.

the ship

How many tons of well-made metal have slid
down the river to the firth, canopied with gulls,
baptized with bands, bottles, shouts, caps in the air?
Deeper and deeper dredgers gave the hulls
leave to carry Glasgow craftwork — where?
Hong Kong and Sidney, Hamburg, Montevideo —
sailors in hammocks, riveters in box beds,
both dreaming of hard knocks, good times ahead.
    Within its forest the ship grows
    tended by hands, jokes, oaths
    and the pride of the bright sparks
    you see flashing their messages
    to the seagoing ages.

EDWIN MORGAN

**Image by
Jan Nimmo**
*Designer and
printer of textiles
selling worldwide.*

SEPTEMBER

Doors Open Day

1 SEPT
CITYWIDE

In 1990, Glasgow will become the first city in Britain to hold a **Doors Open Day.** Over sixty buildings, many of them not normally accessible to the public, will be open to visitors. Buildings – public and private, industrial and ecclesiastic, domestic and commercial – have been chosen because of their style and social significance.

Guides, leaflets and trail maps will help the visitor or enthusiast to make the most of this unique event. A wide number of architectural and public bodies will co-operate to make the day a success. Many of the venues will be mounting special events of their own – ranging from photographic exhibitions to special concerts.

Glasgow Women's Festival

1 TO 30 SEPT
CITYWIDE

Throughout September, Glasgow hosts an ambitious and comprehensive celebration of women's culture. It's an event offering several activities and projects every day – a festival of choices.

There will be a full programme of dance, music and drama workshops. This includes the **Magdalena Project**, an international women's performance workshop, a season of films in association with Glasgow Film Theatre, and 7:84 Theatre Company perform a new play by Rona Munro.

The Wicked Ladies Company stages a new theatrical piece by Aileen Ritchie. And there will also be performances of commissioned works in dance. Literary events include feminist poetry readings and a book festival. The central focus for debate is provided by the **Women and the Arts** conference, four days of keynote speeches, and panel discussion.

wimmin

ELAINE C. SMITH

**Article by
Elaine C. Smith**

*One of Glasgow's
best loved
television, radio and
stage performers.*

'A few days ago the
wife of a
journeyman weaver
was delivered of
three boys, who are
all likely to do well.
What is
remarkable, the
woman has been
eight years
married, and never
had a child before.'
(5 December 1789)

'Johne Kar is fund
in the wrang and
amarciament of
court for turbulens
done be him to
Katerane Hart in
streking of hir
upon the mouthe
with ane salmont
fishe and dome
gewin thairupone'.
(29 May 1576)

**When Glasgow was first named Cultural Capital of Europe
for 1990 my first reaction was one of happiness.**

But as time has gone on, in true Glaswegian fashion, I've had
reservations. I've worried that instead of changing the image from the old
macho-industrialized one we were simply changing it to the macho-
cultural one. The voice and place of women seemed to be ignored – much
as in the rest of society! I'm pleased to say that many women and the 1990
organizers themselves recognized the omission and have set about
planning at least a month's events in September to ensure that women's
art, writing, and dance, are all given a chance to be seen. Throughout the
year, with shows like *The Guid Sisters* and *The Steamie* women will be
very visible. That's a great step forward. Yet, to arrange something as
massive as a year of cultural events is to set yourself up for all kinds of
criticism. If the entire year is too community based or parochial in its
content then the culture vultures from all over Europe will cut it dead and
say that it's impossible for Glasgow, or Scotland, to stage such an event.

On the other hand if the year is too avant-garde in its approach and we
have our theatres full of East German opera, Chinese acrobats and Danish
dance, then the pundits will love it, but the punters won't. Every anarchist/
syndicalist/Trotskyist/Maoist in the area may say it's a festival just for the
rich. And rightly so – we've had too many years of being ignored to stage
a festival that has nothing to do with the real people.

One festival, though, however wonderful, will never solve all the problems
of poverty, unemployment, drug abuse and damp housing or heal the
differences in our society. It is understandable that a wee 'wummin' in
Toryglen is bemused when she sees a concert hall being built by the
District Council yet the windows in her council flat cannot be repaired or
replaced. It is difficult to explain that even if the concert hall and Glasgow
1990 weren't happening repairs still wouldn't be done. It's a question of
priorities and political will – which this present government is exercising
in its own particular way! Fixing damp or repairing windows don't bring
investment – cultural events do.

And because they do – and because we all need events in our lives – we
must welcome and look forward to 1990 and the hope that it brings.
The hope that people will participate, and the hope that the true face of
Glasgow with all its flaws will be reflected for the world to see. I have
always believed that it's 'truth' that people respond to and not an image.
In all things artistic, the true face is what counts.

But it's mostly hope that I, as a woman, wish for the city and its people in
1990 – for hope is what this city and its people deserve.

**Image by
Scot Doran**

*'Glasgow gives me a
sense of belonging
to something
special.'*

Article by
Tom Shields
Glasgow Herald
journalist since
Founded Cultur
City magazine,
May 1987.

a 1990 diary

TOM SHIELDS, Diary Editor of the *Glasgow Herald*, envisages a typical day in the life of Glasgow 1990:

8 am:

In true European fashion, the day starts with breakfast in one of the City of Culture's many cafés. The croissant has become a popular petit déjeuner, especially the filled croissant or, as we say in Glasgow, 'a croissant on'. Most popular is the croissant on black pudding.

9 am:

Time to consult the *Glasgow Herald's* comprehensive listing guide and choose the first cultural foray of the day. Glasgow in Stitches – an exhibition that sounds interesting as well as traditionally Glaswegian. But when I get to the casualty department at the Royal Infirmary, no one seems to have heard of Glasgow in Stitches. Further enquiries reveal that the exhibition is not about the gangs that Glasgow used to have in the bad old days but is a giant community embroidery initiative, based at the Kelvingrove galleries. It is a series of twelve hangings, Glasgow's very own *Bayeux* tapestry I am told. Who is that bloke on the white horse?

10 am:

Out to Chateau du Lait, as the arrondissement of Castlemilk has been renamed for 1990, for an exhibition of cartoons under the banner See Glasgow, See Culture. It is described as a collection of works by 'twenty odd cartoonists'. I see that wee Malky McCormick is involved so the description is pretty accurate. The touring exhibition is giving local would-be artists a chance to disprove such putdowns as 'Him a cartoonist? He couldny draw the dole.'

11 am:

Time to get high. Not a visit to the pub, but a look at the Kite Festival. Kites of all shapes and sizes will be flown. There will be an attempt on the world record of flying 500 kites simultaneously. Me? I'm trying to lose my kite for 1990.

12 noon:

Off to the Tramway Theatre for the Asian bazaar. 1990 will see at least three ethnic festivals – Jewish and Chinese in addition to this Asian event. The bazaar will have hundreds of stalls displaying textiles, arts and crafts, and food. It gives a whole new meaning to the Glasgow phrase 'a big souk'.

2 pm:

Take in a matinee performance of *The Ship*. This is a drama documentary celebrating the great traditions of shipbuilding on the Clyde. The cast includes twenty actors and twelve real shipyard workers. You can tell the real shipyard workers. They have all the funny lines and leave halfway through the performance for a strike meeting in Govan Town Hall. The cast actually make a wee ship during each performance. Well, the actors make the ship. The shipyard workers make three coffee tables, a garden shed, and a standard lamp which they smuggle out of the theatre in their piece boxes.

4 pm:

Time for a look at Dressing the City. Has this event been included because Pat Lally, the leader of the City Council, is a tailor to trade? No it has nothing to do with schmutter; it is a series of murals, painted buses, lorries, and gable ends. Bob Palmer, head of the Festivals Unit, announces a new competition with a prize for whoever finds the bit of Glasgow which has not been painted by the end of 1990.

5 pm:

1990 is The Year of the Horse in the Chinese calendar and to mark this the city has mounted an exhibition on these proud beasts in all their manifestations. It is a concept which thousands of Glaswegians have espoused with some vigour. They flock after work to such venues as Mecca, Ladbrokes, and William Hill to further their studies of these noble animals asking questions like 'Who won the 4.45 at Wincanton?'

6 pm:

A quick look-in at the Glasgow Concert Hall to see if everything is in order for tonight's gala opening. It looks as if the city's administration will achieve its claim that the GICH, Glasgow International Concert Hall (as the hall is to be called) will be ready. What great teamwork as Councillor Jean McFadden and the Lord Provost tack up the hem on the safety curtain while Pat Lally and Bob Gray hoover the red carpet for the Royal visitors.

.30 pm:
Glasgow's new concert hall opens on time. Michael Tumelty, music critic of the *Glasgow Herald*, who has spent two years complaining about the acronym GICH, finally comes to love it since it allows him to write in his first review: 'The GICH opened last night without a hitch.'

10 pm:
Glasgow is all lit up. No, you fool, not another reference to the pubs but to the grand parade of lanterns. More than 10,000 people in a solid stream of light, carrying lanterns of all shapes and sizes. Some of the lanterns are huge and are carried on the backs of lorries. Wee Willie Winkie doesn't have a look-in. And none of the bairns are in their beds, though it's past eight o'clock. They're all having too much fun.

11 pm:
A visit to one of the less pleasant sights in Glasgow 1990: the transit camps which have been set up to give shelter to the thousands of Londoners and Home Counties people who have fled to the city in search of a better quality of life. Some of them will have to wait up to a year before their waterfront flats will be ready.

12 midnight:
Time for a spot of supper at my favourite restaurant, The Omnipresent Fritter, where I witness an uncharacteristic scene of violence. Police have to be called in to separate two men who have come to blows after a furious argument over whether to have the Muscat de Beaume de Venise or the Chateau Yquem with their pudding. This sort of thing has become all too prevalent in Glasgow 1990.

1 am:
Time to visit one of Glasgow's late-night festival clubs. Tonight it is at the Grand Ole Opry as part of the Country Music Festival. The music is by Dwight Yokum and the Judds. 'A pretty strange name,' I venture. Shuggie Two Rivers and the Gringo Kid (the meanest gunslinger in Garthamlock) agree with me.

2 am:
The day ends, as it began, at the Royal Infirmary with a visit to the Stendhal Syndrome Unit. Stendhal Syndrome is the medical name for the condition which arises from an over-exposure to culture (as suffered by the French writer of that name on a visit to Florence a century ago). The symptoms are dizziness from seeing and hearing too many moments of beauty. Ambulances have been shuttling victims all day to the Royal Infirmary from Kelvingrove, the GICH, and other venues. A team of skilled doctors and nurses (the world experts on Stendhal Syndrome) treat the victims by keeping them in darkened rooms and playing Sydney Devine tapes and reading from the collected columns of Jack McLean. The recovery rate is excellent. Many of the patients are able to leave the unit the next morning, fortified by a croissant on fried egg and tattie scone and a glass of Perrier, and are perfectly fit for another day in Glasgow 1990.

SEPTEMBER

Tae Kwon-do

2 SEPT
KELVIN HALL

Teams from sixteen countries, including current World Champions, England, compete in this highly disciplined Korean sport. For the first time women will be included in the teams which now consist of three women and six men and will involve world champions John Kirkwood and David Murphy.

New Music World

5 TO 9 SEPT
TRAMWAY/CITYWIDE

New Music World begins with a programme of live music throughout the city and features bands of varying nationalities, styles and status. The opening and closing nights will be marked with gigs by big names. In between, there will be concerts by some of the most interesting and forward-thinking bands from around the world.

Then comes the **New Music World Seminar**, made up of discussion and question sessions. These will tackle issues such as the implications of the European Market, promotion, training and stage music policy. Finally, **New Music World** brings together a mass of stalls, audio and video displays in a trade exhibition.

The Ship

15 SEPT TO 27 OCT
(REDUCED PRICE PREVIEWS 10 TO 14 SEP)

One of the great events of 1990! At its height, Glasgow was building or repairing an average of thirteen ships a day. **The Ship** is a theatrical tribute to the greatness of the shipbuilding industry in the west of Scotland. The city has commissioned Bill Bryden, associate director of the National Theatre, and William Dudley, award-winning stage designer, to mount this special →

putting on the style

Image by
Michael Kuzmak
'I wouldn't work anywhere else!'

EARL OF GLASGOW

Article by
10th Earl of Glasgow, Patrick Robin Archibald Boyle

Television director/ producer.

Sketch by Alistair Blair,

an adventurer in fashion.

In 1700, Glasgow was generally regarded as one of the most attractive cities in Europe. It was a Cathedral City of some 12,000 people. Even with that relatively small population, it was the second largest city in Scotland, second only to Edinburgh. It was also a University town, the second town in Scotland to have a university, founded in 1453, after St Andrews, but before Edinburgh.

In those days, of course, there was no heavy industry and the Clyde was unpolluted and one of Scotland's finest salmon rivers. It was a town of merchants and craftsmen and prospered on trade, particularly tobacco, which it imported from the American Colonies.

Daniel Defoe, author of *Robinson Crusoe,* was in Glasgow during this period spying for the English government. He wrote:

'Glasgow is indeed a very fine city: the four principal streets are the fairest for breadth, and the finest built that I have ever seen in one city together. The houses are all of stone and generally equal and uniform in height, as well as in front: the lower storey generally stands on vast square dorick columns, not round pillars, and arches between give passage into the shops, adding to the strength as well as the beauty of the buildings. In a word 'tis the cleanest and beautifullest and best built city in Britain, London excepted.'

Since the early eighteenth century, Glasgow has passed through the Industrial Revolution, grown to be the largest city in Scotland and the centre of the fourth largest conurbation in Britain. It changed from being a city whose wealth was based on tobacco to one based on shipbuilding and heavy engineering. Until recently it was the only city outside London to have its own underground railway and, during the first half of this century, prided itself on being the Second City of the Empire.

It reached a low point in the 1930s, when it gained the reputation of being cramped and dirty and 'the Gorbals' became synonymous with the worst slums in Europe. Visitors touring Scotland in the fifties made a special point of avoiding Glasgow. →

Balloch-born in 1959, Blair found glamour in Glasgow, in Christmas shopping, at the pantomime and at the circus at Kelvin Hall.

Blair learnt that commerce was sound in movement, people choosing and bearing packages of various shapes and sizes.

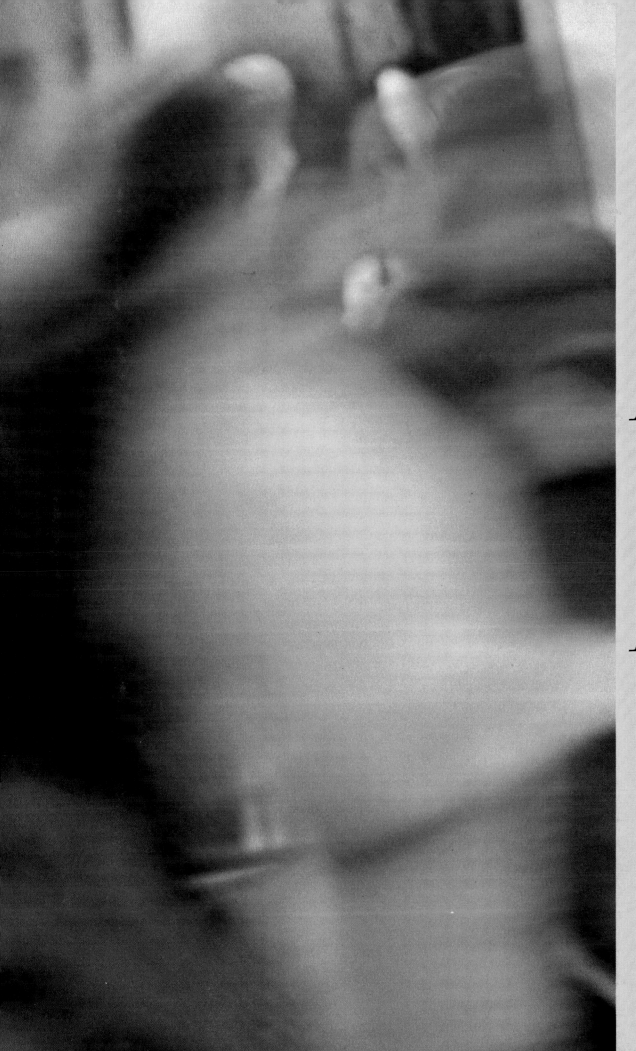

production. Music is being composed by
John Tamms. The cast will include twenty of
Scotland's top actors. They'll perform
alongside ten shipyard workers – welders,
riveters, joiners, platers – who each evening
will build and launch a ship, The Princess of
the Fleet.

To find the right location for this massive
production, every working and redundant
care and maintenance yard on the upper
and lower Clyde has been explored, derelict
factories and warehouses investigated.
Final choice of venue to be announced.

Tom McKendrick

15 SEPT TO 20 OCT
COLLINS GALLERY

Clydebank born artist Tom
McKendrick, whose Clydebank Blitz
paintings were the subject of much critical
acclaim, brings us his latest. Titled
Submarine, it is an exhibition of
paintings and ceramic sculptures based on
the scuttling of the German Fleet at Scapa
Flow – with sound effects!

Musica Nova

16 TO 22 SEPT
HENRY WOOD HALL/
CITY HALL

To help mark the triennial **Musica Nova**
programme, the city has offered commissions to leading Scottish composers. It has
assisted groups to present special
programmes. Also, the **International
Computer Music Conference** is being
held in Glasgow this month.

Musica Nova has grown in range and
stature in the eighteen years of its
existence. In 1990, major figures in
contemporary music will be featured. The
Scottish National Orchestra includes a
world première of James MacMillan's new
Piano Concerto, in which Peter Donohoe is
the soloist. The Scottish Chamber
Orchestra also premières Nigel Osborne's
Violin Concerto. **Musica Nova** has →

Alistair Blair

Now, due in part to a thorough clean-up and a very effective piece of advertising hype, Glasgow has established itself in the eyes of the world as a city in the process of a cultural renaissance. Surely no city in Europe has achieved such a radical change of image in such a short time. Now voted the Cultural Capital of Europe for 1990, it seems to have come full circle after a period of some 250 years.

My view of Glasgow is based on a casual acquaintance over many years rather than any intimate knowledge of any part of it. Yet, it seems to me, that, in spite of all the innovations and upheavals, the spirit of Glasgow has not changed that much since the days of the first Earl. And the beauty of its Victorian heritage is at last being rediscovered. It has always been a proud city with great energy and a surplus of entrepreneurial skills.

Now, as then, Glasgow seems to be the product of individualistic businessmen and an aggressively virile working class. Today, Labour councils seem to have established a surprisingly harmonious relationship with the Thatcherite business community, as if common pride in their city transcends politics.

From St Martin's School of Art in London, Blair went to Paris, working at Dior, with Givenchy, at Chloe and with Largerfeld.

Although an aristocracy, a genteel middle class and the traditional 'canny Scot' do exist in and around Glasgow, they seem to have had little influence on its history – in sharp contrast to several Scottish cities in the east. However, you view its merits, there is nothing genteel or 'canny' about forcing a motorway straight through the middle of a city rather than round the edges.

Glaswegians have their own personality. But it is a paradox that a people who had at one time an exaggerated reputation for violent crime and vomiting drunkenness on Saturday night, can really be so warm, friendly and genuinely concerned for strangers as well as for each other. At the same time, they have a pronounced inferiority complex, particularly towards the English, and a humour that is self-depreciating, so that their best jokes are usually against themselves. Glaswegians are very quick and

Blair's success in the cut and thrust of high fashion is a marvel, like Glasgow's impact on him as a boy.

funny, when you can understand what they are saying.

It is my contention that Glasgow has long been the cultural capital of Scotland. Edinburgh has always assumed that honour partly because it is the capital of Scotland and prettier than Glasgow and partly because, for three weeks in the year, it is transformed into the cultural centre of the world. Glaswegians are often suspicious of the word 'culture' because it implies middle-class tastes and Charles Rennie Mackintosh, the 'Glasgow Boys', Sir William Burrell and Scottish Opera, whose home is in Glasgow. But it also means entertainers like Billy Connolly, criminals like Jimmy Boyle and buskers and robotic dancers in Argyle Street, even the ethnic rivalry between Celtic and Rangers. Edinburgh is the receptacle of culture whereas Glasgow is the generator of it. Edinburgh is Scotland's Washington where Glasgow is its New York. It is here that things happen and are happening. Glasgow is the creative dynamo.

The first Earl chose Glasgow for his time in 1703, although like me he was not really a part of it. In name, I too am proud to be associated with this city, that may have changed its form in three hundred years but not its spirit.

putting on the style

British Hairdresser of the Year 1986. A stylist and lecturer in hair design.

R I T A   R U S K

'You're no' going out dressed like *that* are you?'

We all defied our parents and said 'Try and stop me!'

Glasgow has the same attitude.

We're a city that loves dressing up. We're not like New Yorkers, or people from LA: we're up front, not laid back. We don't go in for understatement. Glasgow is stylish – it just is, and it always has been. There's a terrific energy for the arts in Scotland, but we've had to struggle more than other cities, so we're very proud of our achievements because they're hard won.

Then there's the west of Scotland climate. Don't knock it. More weather means more clothes. Italians or Californians can wear the same stuff any month of the year, but we have the changing seasons to deal with – and when Glaswegians change their clothes, they take the opportunity to change hair style and everything else as well.

Like the infamous Glasgow audience, Glasgow customers are tough. They know a thing or two about style and, wanting to look their best on a limited budget, they make sure they demand that their hairdresser gives a virtuoso performance. Gone are the days when a stylist could rely on a neat line in patter and a winning personality. The customer in this city now wants service, comfort and expertise. High expectation brings out the best in the artist.

That's one reason why so many of Glasgow's stylists and artists are opting to keep the city as their base.

Last year I almost opened an international training school in London. I was worried that I was getting sentimental about my roots (birthplace, that is). Maybe I should move South? But when so many people are moving *in* to Glasgow, why should I be moving *out*? In fact it made real commercial and creative sense to develop here in Glasgow, so in 1990 the international school will open in the city centre.

The students at that school are from Australia, the Far East, Europe and Scotland. What they are learning is Glasgow Style. They'll take that style back home with them and adapt it for Milan or Sydney – because contrary to popular opinion here, the world is genuinely interested in what's happening in Glasgow.

There *is* a Glasgow style, it's hard to define because it's influenced by the myriad of communities that live here, Italian and Asian and Scottish, and it's open to influences from abroad. It doesn't manifest itself in a single look or uniform, but nor are there any breakaway groups making statements. People in Sauchiehall Street may look different from people in Byres Road or in a southside pub. What they share is confidence and quality: they're all bright, brash and Glasgow.

The city hasn't looked so good for years – grand old buildings spruced up, new ones commanding admiration, people and places dressing up for the big party in 1990.

The Festival itself adds its own magic touch: light shows, fireworks, posters, everything done in Glasgow's inimitable and outward-looking style. The reputation that we in the design world have won for ourselves over recent years will be enhanced, as visitors from every country come and see us looking our best. We already have charisma abroad, we Glaswegians. People love the accent, they're intrigued by Scotland, a small nation with such a high profile, and they want to know more about us.

In the eighties we made our mark, particularly in Youth Culture through bands like Simple Minds, and Wet Wet Wet. The fashion business is only one part of Glasgow's style. It's no accident that Charlene, lead singer with one of our most innovative young bands, Texas, began her international career as one of my most talented trainees and models. It's also no accident that at a recent international hair style award show, as the winning act we had The Three Degrees as support! Art and Design are all about communication, and Glaswegians are known never to be short of words.

'Glasgow has the Money, and Edinburgh has the Culture' probably never was true. It's certainly not true now – we at least have our share of the culture. Trust Glasgow to flaunt it, immodestly but with flair, throughout 1990 and beyond.

SEPTEMBER

commissioned the German composer, Wolfgang Rihm, and will feature the music of John Cage. The BBC Scottish Symphony Orchestra and Paragon Ensemble will also be taking part.

The Steamie
17 **SEPT**
KING'S THEATRE
Wildcat's biggest success returns to Glasgow: Based on the intertwined lives, loves and losses of a group of women in the communal washhouse (The Steamie), it is a lovingly nostalgic recreation of community feeling and shared adversity.

Asian Bazaar
17 **TO 29 SEPT**
TRAMWAY
A living Asian Bazaar will be created at Tramway as a showpiece for Asian art and culture.
Artists from Glasgow's Asian communities will collaborate with musicians, performers and craftspeople from Scotland and abroad. Dyers, potters and instrument makers will be demonstrating their crafts. And there will be a programme of traditional and popular music and dance.
Market stalls, food, exhibitions and textiles will help generate a remarkable atmosphere.

Lille National Orchestra
19 **TO 20 SEPT**
CITY HALL
The Lille National Orchestra is one of the major forces in French orchestral music. The orchestra will spend a week as the guests of Strathclyde Regional Council and will stage workshops, masterclasses and a series of mini-concerts for people served by the Region's education and social work departments. The public concerts will be conducted by Jean-Claude Casadesus, the orchestra's founder.

THE LANTERNS

As days are shortened and leaves are falling,

a festival of lights crosses the dark

and gladdens the heart. Everyone can make

a lantern, bobbing, swaying, jaunty, steady,

papery, pumpkiny, Chinesey, Halloweeny,

hung from the Finnieston crane or held by a mouse.

Brandish them through the streets, show autumn

a thing or two as she slinks to her misty house.

 For this is our own procession

 from the outlands to the centre,

 a dance of lights, a maze of lights

 on foot, on floats, on pole and gantry,

 all ages, races, every profession.

Edwin Morgan

THE MOST 'CULTUREFUEL' LEADING LIGHT SINCE 1818

We're delighted to be a prime sponsor of the Lantern Procession on Saturday 6th October 1990, as it enables us to once again take the lead in lighting the streets of Glasgow. And in doing so, hopefully bring as much joy to the people of Glasgow, as our original street lighting did in 1818, when 'The Glasgow Light Company' finally dispelled the darkness once and for all.

Of course gas street lighting is long a thing of the past (6 October being a sort of exception !), but always taking our lead from those innovative days, we've continued to serve the interests of the community, and now here as prime sponsor, we're very proud to be part of Glasgow 1990 Cultural Capital of Europe.

OCTOBER

Glaswegians by Glaswegians

OCT

CITYWIDE

This month sees the opening of a photographic exhibition which has been two years in the making. Cranhill Arts Project has surveyed Glaswegians at work, rest and play all over the city. The exhibition will be staged in the city centre, with simultaneous showings of smaller ones throughout Glasgow. The survey, exhibition and archive will be a legacy for Glaswegians — a reminder of how the city and its people look today. This is said to be the biggest photographic project ever to take place in Scotland. Cranhill will also be mounting a number of smaller exhibitions in a high street photography shop. The first is The Crawfords of Kinning Park. These are family photographs, accumulated over the years. They document typical Glaswegian life in the forties and fifties as seen through the eyes of one family.

The Mod

1 TO 31 OCT

VARIOUS

An Comunn Gaidhealach once again bring **The National Mod** to its favourite venue. Last here during the Garden Festival, **The Mod** is not only a celebration of Gaelic language and culture but also a testing time for aspirants to the various traditional titles. Ceud mille failte do Glaschu 1990!

Lanterns

6 OCT

CITYWIDE

Lanterns involves thousands of participants from Glasgow and Strathclyde. Schools, community groups, art centres, businesses, workforces in their workplaces, drama groups and clubs: all of these have worked with a team of visual artists over a →

Glasgow District Council

Glasgow international concert hall

JIM WAUGH

**Article by
Jim Waugh**
Broadcasts and
writes on jazz, has
introduced many
listeners to jazz.

Glasgow's new International Concert Hall, (to be opened in October) will be one of the best venues of its kind in the United Kingdom, and one which will have few rivals in Europe for facilities or ambitious planning.

The building stands proudly at the top of Buchanan Street, its two halves fixed south and west.

The view to the west takes in some of the great treasures of Glasgow architecture: Mackintosh's School of Art, the Gilmorehill campus of Glasgow University and, in the distance, the mountains of the Trossachs.

Construction has been comparatively swift, although the idea is more than twenty years old. In just over two years there has grown one of the most complex and highly finished buildings of its kind.

Today every new construction must take into account the probability of widely varying use. The Glasgow International Concert Hall is a model of such contemporary adaptability.

'I was vexed to hear that there is some thought of giving me the freedom of Glasgow in a gold box. This may make it necessary for me to make a speech on which I had not reckoned.'
(Thomas Babington MacCauley, before being elected Lord Rector of Glasgow University, 1848)

The first dozen or so rows of the stalls emerge from beneath the stage and slide easily into place. The stage itself expands to accommodate a full symphony orchestra and, behind them, there is space for a full choir. When the transformation is complete, the main auditorium can hold almost 2,500, making it the largest of its kind in Britain. And yet, by some architect's magic, it is one of the most intimate of venues.

When Jessye Norman smiles at Sir Alexander Gibson before unrolling that majestic voice of hers on 14 November, everyone in the hall will feel as if he or she could reach out and shake her hand. When Oscar Peterson is next in Glasgow, every jazz fan will be convinced that they could lean forward and play 'Chopsticks' in duet. When the next major snooker tournament comes to Glasgow, everyone will hear the click of the winning pot.

Surrounding this heart of the building is a series of supporting foyers, exhibition spaces, a conference hall which can hold 500 and a restaurant for 300. The shopping centre which is an integral and crucial part of the whole scheme has its first layers below the concert hall.

The Glasgow International Concert Hall is a place for the people of Glasgow (and their visitors) to enjoy the very best in all kinds of entertainment.

PLAYING A SUPPORTING ROLE ALL OVER SCOTLAND.

OCTOBER

period of eighteen months. They have made lanterns, lanterns of all shapes and sizes, for a huge celebration of light in the autumn of 1990.

The team of artists, led by John Fox of Welfare State International, Engineers of the Imagination, are preparing simple hand-held lanterns made of withy and tissue. They are also making bigger ones — to be carried on the back, or by several people. And even bigger ones — to be suspended in the street, or on buildings. And giant lanterns will be constructed for the backs of trucks and lorries. Large groups from all over Strathclyde will provide music of all kinds to accompany the lanterns. At the climax of the project lanterns and makers take to the streets for a series of night processions converging on George Square.

Whistler in Europe Exhibition

6 OCT TO 5 JAN 1991
HUNTERIAN ART GALLERY

'James McNeil Whistler was a mystery' starts the preface to Catherine A. Lockman's authoritative book on Whistler and it is hoped that this exhibition will cast some light on the European influences on his work from his student days in Paris to his later sojourns in Venice, Amsterdam and Corsica. Go along and see why he is hailed as the greatest printmaker since Rembrandt. There are pastels and drawings as well as prints.

Glasgow International Concert Hall

8 OCT
GLASGOW INTERNATIONAL CONCERT HALL

The most important permanent legacy of 1990 — Glasgow's new international concert hall — opens on 8 October. This magnificent new 2,500 seat venue is a landmark in the city's and Scotland's musical history. The opening programme is →

city of escape

**Article by
Tom Weir**

Journalist and photographer, author of books on climbing and Scotland.

TOM WEIR

Sixty years ago when I took to the hills that are everywhere around Glasgow I was not the only working lad discovering how easy it was to get out of the city at cheap cost. The tramways had a book of good walks from every terminus. By changing at Dalmuir you could get to Loch Lomond. The railways offered every kind of cheap excursion, an evening trip to the source of the Clyde. On summer Sundays Mallaig was only 9/- return. Using the Oban line you could have a train and boat excursion, on Loch Tay from Killin, or on Loch Awe from its station. On the Clyde paddle steamers competed with each other for trade; yes and there could be bands playing on deck!

I lived in Springburn then, the highest part of Glasgow, which could boast that it was the locomotive building empire of Europe employing an élite labour force of over ten thousand men. The tenement block where I lived at the bend of the road was within easy distance of four of the largest railway works in Britain.

The majority of families were housed like us, in lines of tenements, three storeys high, with three families to a landing, sharing a common toilet a half-stair down. One room and kitchen was the norm, and in ours were housed my mother, grandmother, brother and sister. My father who had been an engine fitter, was killed in action in Mesopotamia just fifteen months after I was born. To supplement her widow's pension my mother worked as a wagon painter in Cowlairs.

There was plenty to interest a boy in Springburn. It had five cinemas, swimming-baths, a fine public park, backcourts to the tenements with washhouses offering challenging jumps from one to the other.

There was also the Springburn Amateur Boxing and Wrestling Club with rings, mats, weight-lifting equipment and a fine bunch of railway men to teach you techniques. It was a time too when cycling was a pleasure on roads where motor cars were relatively few. There was no holding me in Springburn once I got a bike and could go off exploring the countryside on my own.

The tenement block where I lived at the bend of the road was within easy distance of four of the largest railway works in Britain.

As Johnson had done in October 1773, Wordsworth, his sister Dorothy and Coleridge stayed at the Saracen's Head in Gallowgate, 1803. 'I never saw anything like the Falls of Clyde. It would be a delicious spot to have near one's own house.'
(From Dorothy Wordsworth's Diary 1803)

Wild grey geese from Iceland fly into the Loch Lomond Nature Reserve. Tom Weir.

Ross Connelly Primary

I began searching the libraries for books on mountaineering and determined that I was going to be an explorer and see these marvellous bits of Scotland I was reading about.

It is no accident that the very first club devoted to serious climbing was the Scottish Mountaineering Club. It was formed in 1889 as a result of a letter to the *Glasgow Herald* on 10 January of that year. At its first Annual Dinner, held in the Grand Hotel, Glasgow, Professor George Ramsay, its first President said in his speech to thirty members present: 'Gentlemen, the marvel is not that our Club is formed, but that it was not formed before. The love of scenery and of hills is implanted in the hearts of every Scot as part of his very birthright; our mountains have been the moulders of our national character...'

The founders of the Scottish Mountaineering Club were professional men of great resource, with enough time and money to put their leisure to good use, exploring the hills and glens in summer and winter in a detailed way that had never been done before. Mine was the first generation of working-class mountaineers, and by 1939, one of the most outstanding of professional class climbers wrote in compliment to them:

'... the new group of climbers find themselves not so much heirs to a tradition as the discoverers of a secret hitherto kept hidden from their class.'

More typical today is a youthful pair starting out late, after making breakfast, from their tent or youth hostel which they reached late the previous night. Some are members of the JMCS or the Lomond or Creagh Dhu Clubs. Some of them climb every weekend of the year. They appear to me to have the future of Scottish climbing in their hands.'

The man who was to be my lifelong companion I met on the Fort William train: Matt Forrester, red haired and six feet tall, was a butcher, with the same shop-hours as myself, so it was Saturday evening last-buses or trains that took us to places we had never been. There was also the Craigallion Fire: here we would meet working men, slightly older than ourselves who seemed to have been everywhere. It was a kind of Open

University of knowledge of the great outdoors within easy walking distance of Milngavie tram terminus.

Jock Nimlin was one of the great names of that time. He had been camping and climbing since 1928, and although he worked in a shop until 9 p.m. on Saturdays, for years he was never known to spend a weekend at home. He died just over a year ago. Talking of these early days with him I recalled him saying:

'Aye, these were weekends of simplicity I would not have missed. At that period of the early thirties just to have a job was happiness. Yet people had hopes for the future. We discussed Utopias and political solutions. Climbing was a healthy outlet. We did it for adventure, sleeping in caves, like tramps using newspapers as blankets.'

What happened to the Craigallion Fire? Delightfully placed, in a hollow by a loch, sheltered by a pinewood and backed by the steep front of the Campsies we loved it. In Matt's diary, passed to me after his death at fifty-eight years of age, he had written of the fire: 'Coming along the track of a winter's evening, the glow of light and the merry shouts of laughter brought joy to the heart. One could always be assured of company there, good company, and pleasant tales of the countryside.'

Alas the popularity of the cult of hiking put an end to Craigallion. The fire was banned by the landowner because of litterlouts and despoilers hacking down living trees.

Everything changes, forty years on all the houses where I once delivered milk are down. Springburn Road is now an Express Way with a new road system, bewildering to those who knew its streets in the days of its greatness. New buildings are arising, many of its soot-surfaced tenements have been cleaned to reveal their pink stone-work; urban renewal goes on apace. There is every hope that a new community will arise – a fitting tribute to the craftsmen who built and serviced these mastodons of pre-history, the steam locomotive, and a fitting start to a new century, speeded on its way by the events of 1990.

OCTOBER

a foretaste of its future contribution to concert-going in Glasgow.

The hall will be the Scottish National Orchestra's new home. The SNO gives the opening public concert on 8 October — featuring special commissions from Thomas Wilson and Thea Musgrove. A special performance of Mahler's **Symphony No. 8** takes place one week later.

For the rest of the year, the orchestra's weekly subscription seasons will continue — supplemented by special concerts and regular appearances by the Scottish Chamber Orchestra, the BBC Scottish Symphony Orchestra, and the recently established Glasgow Philharmonic Orchestra. The hall will also present leading names and attractions in light entertainment. A series of visiting orchestras of world repute follows the opening of the hall. These include the **Berlin Philharmonic** in two concerts (9, 10 Oct), the **Bolshoi Orchestra** (12 Oct), the **Orchestra of the Age of Enlightenment** (16 Oct), the **London Philharmonic** (30 Oct), the **Leipzig Gewandhaus** in a three-concert Brahms cycle (31 Oct, 1, 2 Nov), the **Israel Philharmonic** (21 Nov), and the **Orchestre de Paris** (Dec). The number and standard of guest orchestras is a first in Glasgow's history, and full repertoire details will be published soon. The concerts will give special place to the work of Gustav Mahler, whose Fifth, Sixth, Seventh and Eighth symphonies will be performed during the opening season. All booking opens 2 April.

The (Inter)national Review of Live Art

9 TO 14 OCT
THIRD EYE CENTRE/TRAMWAY

One of the more radical events of 1990 is the tenth **National Review of Live Art.** This annual season is recognized as →

Image by
Fiona Burnell
*'After graduation in
1991, I want to
spread the news
about Glasgow
design throughout
the world'.*

transports of delight

C L I F F   H A N L E Y

Article by
Cliff Hanley
*Writer and
broadcaster, famous
for his wit and
perception of
Scottish life.*

Take a ride on a tuppenny tram

And happy you will be

From daylight till dark

There's many a park

Just waiting for you and me

Don't spend your hoard

On a Daimler or Ford

Like the workers of Uncle Sam

Since Mister Dalrymple made

motoring simple

With Glasgow's tuppenny tram

**So they sang away (see left) back between the wars.
Dalrymple was Glasgow's transport director, and tuppence
wasn't a lot of money even in those days.**

But the Tram was merely one chapter in a long history of transport,
because the Glaswegian has always been an incurable traveller.

Ten centuries ago they were probably wandering Picts who took a fancy to
the broad meandering Clyde and were prepared to settle and wait for a
century and a half for the building of Glasgow Cathedral.

In the nineteenth century there was a flood from Ireland, escaping from
potato famines and other irritations, and from the Scottish Highlands,
where a project wittily called The Improvements had made a clearance of
the crofters.

By that time the Clyde was one of the world's busiest waterways. The
steamboat had arrived, first with the *Charlotte Dundas* on the Forth and
Clyde Canal, and then, in 1812, with Henry Bell's *Comet*. He didn't 'invent'
the steamboat, of course. He was merely a farsighted businessman who
got somebody to build a hull to fit an engine.

Other local entrepreneurs saw the sense in steam, and within a few years
there were a couple of dozen steamers plying from the Broomielaw.

There were occasional disasters. The first *Comet* ran aground to
destruction, her successor had a head-on crash with another boat and
sank with nearly all hands. Boilers burst now and then, vessels sank or
ran aground. None of that could quench Glasgow's lust for sailing.

Throughout this century, till well after the Second World War, the Clyde
paddlers were in the city's blood, and for most keelies, a holiday *meant* a
trip doon the watter. In its way, Glasgow pioneered the working-class
holiday. →

Tom Weir

'A quarter of a million people gather to wave goodbye to Glasgow's last tramcars.'
(Daily Record, 5 September, 1962.)

**First direct mail
coach London-
Glasgow arrived at
the Saracen's
Head 7 July 1788.**

OCTOBER

the platform for experimental performance-based work in Britain. Productions commissioned or premièred during 1988 included DV8's outstanding Dead Dreams of Monochrome Men, the third part of Man Act's trilogy, and works by Geraldine Pilgrim, Stephen Taylor Woodrow, and Annie Griffin. In 1990, the National Review becomes international, featuring European groups and artists of outstanding creativity. There will also be an opportunity for young Scottish artists and groups to showcase their work during the season.

Youth Olympiad

18 TO 21 OCT
KELVIN HALL

The Olympiad is similar to a mini Olympic Games. Athletes are aged fourteen years or under — and compete at district level. Ten countries plus the home team will compete in a dozen sports, from handball to Tae Kwon-do, from basketball to badminton.

Expect all the excitement and atmosphere of a major sporting occasion for four days. The opening and closing ceremonies are set to be something special too.

Paragon Ensemble

28 OCT
ROYAL SCOTTISH ACADEMY OF MUSIC & DRAMA, STEVENSON HALL

Scotland's leading contemporary music ensemble celebrates its tenth anniversary in fine style with a concert which includes works by Busoni, Debussy and Mahler. High point of the evening will be the world première of the work by Benedict Mason, winner of this year's Paragon Prize for Composition. Under the direction of founder David Davies, the Paragon has lived up to its name. It is one of the prime commissioners of new works in Scotland and has received the warmest praise in its several tours in England and Europe.

When a train wanted to move, it seized the cable with a clamp and was yanked along.

Tom Weir

Latterly, the steamers were run by the rival companies LMS (a yellow band on the funnel) and LNER (red bands) and the passengers joined in the rivalry, yelling to their captain to win the race to the next pier. The timber uprights of the Clyde piers took a terrible thrashing, because the boats were almost unsteerable with all the passengers crowded at the shoreward rails and the whole thing tilted thirty degrees off the vertical, with the offshore paddle whirling in mid air.

Time moved on, of course, citizens found fresh transports in packages to the Mediterranean, and the Clyde seemed set for a decline. The proud paddlers are replaced by workaday diesel ferries for people and cars. But the Firth is coming back into fashion in an age when a foreign holiday can include weekends spent trying to sleep on airport floors.

And of course, one old glory remains, in the shape of the venerable *Waverley*, the lovingly-restored paddler that takes sentimental enthusiasts in their hordes from up-river to the magic waters.

There is another, of course. Glasgow's subway refuses to go away, has face-lifts instead. It began with rope traction. A hefty rope ran round the wall constantly pulled along by a hidden pulley engine. When a train wanted to move, it seized the cable with a clamp and was yanked along. When it wanted to stop, it let go and applied the brake.

Suddenly the sheer speed of the trains got the air whirling, pure, clean and cool...

The air was pretty stale down there, but our forefathers were hardened to stale air. Electrification brought a dramatic change. Suddenly the sheer speed of the trains got the air whirling, pure, clean and cool and on Glasgow's occasional days of torrid sunshine, citizens would linger at the top of the subway steps to bask and breathe.

And in the heyday of the tramcar, that noble artefact was for holidays as well as workaday transport. It certainly helped to spread the city, when workers realized they no longer had to live above the shop but could move out to breathe air far from the shipyard grime.

...whole conurbation unfolding beside them as they ate their picnic sandwiches and drank their lemonade...

The management had the engaging idea of permitting schoolchildren to travel any distance on one line for a penny during school holidays. A couple of youngsters could board a tram in the Near East, like Shettleston, go all the way to the Airdrie terminus, then take another penny ride to Ferguslie Mills and be left with another cheap fare back home.

In simple terms of mileage, they were getting the equivalent of a trip almost as long as a journey to Edinburgh and back, with a whole conurbation unfolding beside them as they ate their picnic sandwiches and drank their lemonade (usually finished within the first mile, of course).

In the grip of the passion for modernization, the city abandoned the beloved trams and in a sense, a society vanished. The old trams of the thirties had little five-seat compartments upstairs at front and back, and it was possible to sit in the front compartment and have interesting chats with the driver downstairs. He enjoyed a blether.

Modern times are inevitable, at any point in history. So it is goodbye to the tram and hello to the omnibus.

But the city triumphantly clings to the modernized past in its freshened suburban railway system, a long and cherished history brought up to date. The suburban railways were always wildly romantic. Young commuters had the time and the peace to talk. Some, wildly daring, even talked to fellow-travellers of the other sex, and sometimes one thing led to another. Ah, romance, romance.

We are now talking seriously of light railways in the city connecting with the established network. It could happen. We will keep moving. That is what Glaswegians were born to do.

> *There's Partick Cross and Cessnock*
> *Hillheid and Merkland Street*
> *George's Cross and Govan Cross*
> *Where a' the people meet*
> *West Street, Shields Road, the train goes*
> *round and round*
> *It's lovely going your holidays*
> *On the Glasgow Underground.*
> **Chorus from a Subway-inspired song**

NOVEMBER

November Music
DATES AS BELOW
GICH

Ten outstanding concerts in the concert hall this month. The Scottish National Orchestra's opening season offers Stravinsky and Strauss, conducted by Bamert. Then there's Mozart and Bartok with Rafael Fruhbeck de Burgos. And, on 24 November, Bryden Thomson will conduct the world première of a 1990 commission — Gordon Crosse's new choral work for the SNO and the SNO Chorus.

Visiting orchestras and artists of the highest quality will be in Glasgow. The **Leipzig Gewandhaus Orchestra** gives three concerts and plays a complete cycle of Brahms' four symphonies and two piano concertos. The conductor is Kurt Masur, the soloist is Alfred Brendel (31 Oct, 1-2 Nov).

On 14 November you can hear the BBC Scottish Symphony Orchestra with guest soprano, Jessye Norman. On the 21st, it's the **Israel Philharmonic Orchestra** opening the **Festival of Jewish Culture.** The BBC Scottish Symphony Orchestra gives a **European Broadcasting Union Concert** on 26 November.

Edouard Vuillard
1 TO 30 NOV
WASHINGTON GALLERY

Co-founder with Pierre Bonnard of the group known as The Nabis, Vuillard remains one of the most unique artists of the twentieth century. His portraits and interiors, with their almost obsessive interest in the patterns of wallpaper and carpets, place him as the supreme poet of upholstery and bric-a-brac. This exhibition commemorates the fiftieth anniversary of the artist's death.

Image by
Martin Barnard

'Glasgow is at its best after dark, everywhere I look there is a picture'.

at the movies

J O H N   B R O W N

Article by
John Brown

Screenwriter — The Justice Game and its sequel The Lady from Rome were both based in and around Glasgow city.

The movies? An affectation, surely – don't the Scots talk about going to the pictures?

Not in Glasgow, I was delighted to find when I moved (from the east coast and Another City) to the un-new Glasgow of the early 1970s. People didn't go to the pictures or the cinema, they went to the movies.

The movies mean entertainment of a special kind: the classic Hollywood cinema of the years before and after the Second World War. For some reason, there has always been a unique sympathy for American popular culture in the tastes of Glasgow audiences; Gordon Williams, the Paisley-born novelist, tells of his experience as a young reporter in interviewing stars like Bob Hope, Dean Martin and Jerry Lewis and many others who came to Glasgow to appear at the Empire or Alhambra and found, to their amazement, that their native material had the audiences rolling in the aisles while their specially written 'British' routines fell flat. Glasgow belonged with Chicago, Pittsburgh, Philadelphia and the other great industrialized cities of America rather than with London, Manchester, Birmingham and the tastes of the English.

…they relished another area of Hollywood's output, the often brutal action thrillers and westerns…

So too in the cinemas. The Glasgow audiences welcomed certain kinds of film which were unsure of a reception elsewhere in Britain or indeed Scotland. The fast-paced, wisecracking Hollywood comedies of the forties, fifties and sixties, were reliable fillers of the Odeons and ABCs. I can recall from my own experience in the 1970s the Glasgow reaction to films like *The Owl and the Pussycat* and the Billy Wilder version of *The Front Page*. The audiences clearly adored the metropolitan wit and snap of these, yes, *movies*, just as they relished another area of Hollywood's output, the often brutal action thrillers and westerns featuring stars like Burt Lancaster, Kirk Douglas, Robert Mitchum, Clint Eastwood and Charles Bronson. →

Colin Waddell

NOVEMBER

Jessye Norman and the BBC Scottish Symphony Orchestra

14 NOV
GICH

One of the world's greatest sopranos makes a rare British appearance as part of the opening programme of the new concert hall. Jessye Norman is one of the most popular operatic and platform singers anywhere. She has been seen performing in special events like the Wembley Free Nelson Mandela concert, and the revolutionary happening staged for the Paris Bicentennaire celebrations. Her appearance in Glasgow is a major coup for the BBC SSO.

The repertoire for the concert is likely to include the last scene from Strauss' **Salome,** and a work by Wagner.

The Age of Van Gogh

15 NOV TO 31 JAN 1991
THE BURRELL COLLECTION

Vincent Van Gogh died aged thirty-seven in 1890. On the centenary of his death, Glasgow pays tribute to this European master. There will be a major exhibition of his work, together with paintings by contemporaries, from the period 1880-1895. Organized in collaboration with the Rijksmuseum Van Gogh, Amsterdam, it will be the only show of its kind outside the Netherlands in 1990.

Festival of Jewish Culture

21 NOV TO 2 DEC
ROYAL SCOTTISH ACADEMY OF MUSIC & DRAMA/CITYWIDE

Ten days of Jewish and Israeli cultural events take place in Glasgow between 21 November and 2 December. Musical highlight of the season is the **Israel** →

00111

...a showcase for

non-American

movies, for the best

of European

cinema...

It's possible to detect a strong element of wish fulfilment in these popular tastes. It could be argued that Glasgow audiences – the men in them, at any rate – loved these sorts of movies because they saw in them, an image of a world they admired and wanted to believe that they too inhabited. In *A Sense of Freedom*, John Mackenzie's and Peter MacDougall's mesmerizing television film about Jimmy Boyle, David Hayman's swaggering entry recalls nothing so much as the archetypal appearance of James Cagney in his great gangster roles – a chilling reminder that the influence of popular culture isn't always benign. On the other hand, the quartet of beleaguered but indomitable women in the Glasgow washhouse of Tony Roper's wonderful play *The Steamie* testifies to the positive strength of other Hollywood role models: the disillusioned but enduring personae of stars such as Bette Davis, Rosalind Russell, Joan Crawford and Jean Arthur, women who survived defiantly in a man's world.

But if city audiences love Hollywood at its most Hollywood, there is of course another Glasgow tradition in cinema-going which is equally enthusiastic, to be summed up in one name: Mr Cosmo. In 1939, to the sad shaking of heads amongst his colleagues, George Singleton opened the Cosmo in Rose Street with a French film, Julien Duvivier's *Carnet du Bal*. It was intended as a showcase for non-American movies, for the best of European cinema which had hitherto been available to 'discerning filmgoers' as Singleton saw them through the members-only screenings organized by the Glasgow Film Society. The shaking of heads was commercially motivated: how could such a specialized cinema – what would later become termed an art-house cinema – survive?

Not only did it survive, it flourished, introducing Glasgow audiences to the dazzling range of postwar European cinema, Bergman, Fellini, Renoir, Satyajit Ray, Resnais, Antonioni, Godard, Truffaut, Chabrol and the other young iconoclasts of the French New Wave, all cunningly interwoven with the best English-language films from independent American directors like John Cassavetes and Joseph Strick and the new British directors such as Lindsay Anderson and Karel Reisz. 'Mr Cosmo' proved that 'discerning filmgoers' could be as loyal as those of the Odeons and the ABCs.

Indeed, amongst those flocking to the Cosmo in the fifties and sixties were the future Scottish film-makers of the seventies and eighties – was it during a screening of a Truffaut movie, possibly, that the Gregory of *Gregory's Girl*, Scottish cousin to Jean-Pierre Leaud and Antoine Doinel, was born in Bill Forsyth's head?

Indeed, there are probably more cinema screens in Glasgow now than ever before: no less than forty-one of them in the city centre itself and surrounding areas, and a range of movies on offer which has something for every taste. The Glasgow appetite for movies, all kinds of movies wherever they come from make it especially appropriate that in 1990, the third annual ceremony of the European Film Awards takes place here.

Beginning in Berlin in 1988 and moving on to Paris in 1989, the Awards mark a decisive development on the world cinema scene. The critics have always recognized a European dimension in international film-making, but in the last few years this critical recognition has been translated into economic and political terms. While Hollywood, ever alert to new trends, remakes European movies – *Trois Hommes et un Couffin* becomes *Three Men and a Baby* – European producers and directors have a new sense of identity and common cause in addressing audiences throughout the world, and the European Film Awards form an expression and a celebration of that new awareness.

As a kind of crossroads where the European and American traditions of film audiences meet, there could be no better host than Glasgow in 1990 for this major movie event. →

... for Glasgow 1990
Cultural Capital of Europe.

We're proud to be Prime Sponsors
of this fine exhibition.

another reel – another film

B I L L   F O R S Y T H

**Article by
Bill Forsyth**

*Has directed six
feature films, both
home and abroad.*

I was born in 1946. That year the commercial cinema world-wide reached its historic climax. Attendances were at record levels, never since bettered. I have pursued my work with the irksome knowledge that the year of my birth signalled the start of the decline of the cinema-going habit!

…a European

dimension in

international

film-making.

In the thirties and forties Glasgow was a city intoxicated by cinema. Box-office admissions rivalled those of London. At this time American cinema was carrying out its cultural invasion of all parts of the planet that were serviced by electricity, and Glaswegians were among the most eager of victims.

We were, after all, practically Americans already. Glasgow was an emigrant city, a place that people left. It was a point of departure for the land of promise. Citizens of the city are quite simply the descendants of those who neglected to get on the boat. So we lived a vicarious fantasy life as Americans-who-might-have-been. We embraced the America of the movies warmly.

This intimacy with mythical America could play havoc with an unschooled sense of geography. As a child I imagined the Wild West to be,

correctly, somewhere beyond the western horizon, but mistakenly judged it to be a walk or a cycle ride away. My particular horizon was the Gleniffer Braes above Paisley, which would have placed Tombstone, Arizona somewhere in the region of Johnstone, or perhaps Dunlop.

When it came to imagining a life as a film-maker, then perversely, familiarity with America let us down. Hollywood in the movies was a never-never land. Becoming a film director was so unachievable an ambition that it was barely worth the effort to fantasize. Our predestined role was as the audience.

A further stumbling-block to the growth of home-made narrative cinema was the image that Scotland had appropriated as the natural home of the documentary film, or at least the documentary film-maker. John Grierson's global holy war for the cause of factual cinema helped put this stamp on us. It almost seemed like letting the side down to want to make limp-wristed 'story' films, as opposed to the manly, roughly-tweeded, pipe-smoking documentary films that should be our true calling, and were our birthright.

For decades the only route into the world of theatrical cinema began with the train or bus or aeroplane out of town.

Then came the generation of the stay-at-homes, like myself. By the early seventies the Scottish predilection to leave home at all costs was on the wane. We were becoming more familiar with the outside world, and less romantic about its possibilities.

Scotland seemed at last to be as good a place as any to make a go of things. In film, we found our inspiration not in America but in Europe, in the generation of film-makers, mostly French, called the New Wave. They made their films cheaply, in the streets, in cafés, in apartments. Their films, on the whole, were inventive, fun →

and extremely watchable. It wasn't simply the films that inspired us, but the example of the film-makers themselves. They seemed to be people pretty much like ourselves. They were in their thirties, crazy about movies and determined to make them. They had one advantage over us. They did not share a common language with the United States. Although they cheekily stole from and made constant reference to American movies, they were ultimately free to address their own local audience in their own vernacular.

We were slow on the uptake, but eventually we began to ask ourselves the right questions. If Louis Malle and Francois Truffaut could hit the streets of St Denis or Versaille and make cinema, why couldn't we do the same in Byres Road, or Bridgeton? And remember, we had that huge ready-made audience in Glasgow. Granted, they were conditioned to American formula movie fodder, but surely this slumbering giant of an audience would spring loyally to life at the first sign of some home-grown product.

I used to excite myself with the numbers. A total population in Scotland of five million. But let's be realistic and admit that, for whatever unfathomable reason, a portion of the population *don't* want to see a Scottish film. Let's be outrageously pessimistic and call it fifteen per cent. Let's say a further ten per cent are indisposed or don't have a cinema nearby. What are you left with? In big, round numbers, a potential audience of nearly four million people. And what about the fabled Scots Abroad? Another twenty million at the last reckoning. My heart used to race at the prospect of twenty-four million Scots, at a conservative £2 per head. I began pre-production immediately.

Two years later, without having made a dent in the defences of the few film funding sources in Britain at the time, I came to a conclusion the next best thing to making a film with lots of money is to make a film with no money at all. In Glasgow, there were enough friends and associates in the film business to put together an entire crew. For three weeks, with the young actors from the Glasgow Youth Theatre, we raced around Glasgow making our film, and what was probably more meaningful to us, behaving like real film-makers at last.

Then came the day when the film (*That Sinking Feeling*) was released in its native city. I still remember the thrill of listening to the commercial for it on Radio Clyde. The Glasgow audience did its best, but it wasn't good enough for the moguls in London. After one week our little film vanished from the city cinemas. So much for the twenty-four million. A few weeks later it briefly reappeared at a downtown cinema usually reserved for the dirty raincoat brigade. Then that cinema burnt to the ground, never to reopen. I hope the fact that my film was running at the time was coincidental. You have to be thick-skinned in the film business.

I have thought about it a lot since, and I think I know why our little film didn't quite set the heather afire. Our Glasgow audience stayed away out of a perverse kind of loyalty. They were afraid that the film wouldn't be as good as they wanted it to be, and didn't want to get caught up in the embarrassment of it all. A similar trait surfaced when Dougal Haston became the first Scotsman to ascend Mount Everest. I remember standing in a queue in an all-night shop when the news came through that he was spending the night on the summit. After the initial thrill of vicarious pride rippled around the shop, we were brought back down to earth by a sober pronouncement from someone in the queue. 'That's all very well', he said, 'but he's still got to get back down, hasn't he?' Dougal Haston's moment had come and gone in a twinkling of an eye, mysterious, frustrating and touching. My terror and admiration for it, will keep me close to Glasgow for as long as I live and worry.

What are you left with? In big, round numbers, a potential audience of nearly four million people.

DECEMBER

European Film Prize

2 DEC

GLASGOW INTERNATIONAL CONCERT HALL/GLASGOW FILM THEATRE

All eyes on Glasgow. The prestigious **European Film Prize** comes to the city. An international jury of well-known film personalities will make awards for the most outstanding films, performers, directors and designers during 1990. Europe's television networks will be broadcasting this tribute to European cinema to millions of viewers. The awards ceremony will be accompanied by celebrity lectures, discussions and special screenings of the winning films at the Glasgow Film Theatre.

December Music

7 TO 20 DEC

GLASGOW INTERNATIONAL CONCERT HALL

December brings the BBC Scottish Symphony Orchestra back to the concert hall with a performance of Beethoven's Missa Solemnis, conducted by Leopold Hager (7 Dec). On the 11th, the Scottish National Orchestra and Chorus, Scottish Philharmonic Singers and the Royal Scottish Academy of Music and Drama Choir join forces to perform Berlioz's masterpiece — the **Grande Messe des Morts.** This will be conducted by Philip Ledger, with tenor soloist Anthony Rolfe-Johnson.

The SNO's December concerts include Mahler (Symphony No. 4 and Kindertotenlieder, conducted by Neeme Jarvi), Walter Weller with Salvatore Accardo and, on the 13th and 15th of the month, an all-Elgar programme conducted by Yehudi Menuhin. The programme includes the Violin Concerto.

In a coda to European Cultural Capital year, the **Orchestre de Paris** makes its first visit to Scotland with conductor Semyon Bychkov.

tell it like it is

BILLY KAY

**Article by
Billy Kay**

*Edited two books on
Scottish working-
class oral history.
Author of Scots –
Mither Tongue.*

Some say it's Glesca and some call it Glasgow, some pronounce it Glezga, for others it's Glazgol. As there are many ways of pronouncing the name of the city, there are many varieties of Glasgow speech.

These may reflect directly the social class of the speaker, and in a more subtle way even the person's religion or regional origin of his or her parents. There is however a recognizable Glasgow dialect – a potent blend of Lowland Scots and contemporary English and American, with a pinch of Irish and Scottish Gaelic thrown in. Not every Glaswegian speaks it – Scottish Standard English is widely spoken by the city's middle class – but all are influenced by it. For whereas in Edinburgh the working classes are defined by the culture of the more linguistically Anglicized middle classes, in Glasgow the opposite prevails and the professional classes have some of the street wisdom and gallousness of the predominant working-class ethos of the city.

The result of this is that everyone from Glasgow is recognizably Scottish in speech. 'The Patter' is the term of endearment Glasgow folk have for the raciest, wittiest forms of their language. Inside every Glaswegian there is a 'patter merchant' desperate to get out, and even socially-mobile Glasgow yuppies know that the power of the patter lies in judicious use of the dialect. You hear it everywhere. It has tremendous street credibility in the city. Through the popularity of Glasgow comedians and detectives on television, it has recently gained popularity outwith the city as well.

I say recently, for when Glasgow used to suffer the false media stereotypes of slum housing, poverty and violence, the dialect was associated with all of this and dismissed as corrupt patois and debased urban slang. Glasgow folk of course knew the humanity and the warmth of the folk who spoke the dialect and could ignore the medias clichés. What did get to them however, was the rubbishing of their speech in their education. Told to 'talk properly' by their teachers, like most Lowland Scots they became totally bi-lingual.

The result of this can be disconcerting for an outsider interested in local dialects – you may overhear it but rarely hear it spoken directly to you. In a restaurant, for example, someone may say to you, 'Wid ye gie me ower yin o thay spuins, please?' But if you look blank, the question will instantly be transformed before your very ears to, 'Would you give me over one of those spoons, please?' Because of this underground quality of all Scots dialects – now you hear them, now you don't – I sometimes liken their use to illicit sexual acts – indulged in by consenting adults in the privacy of their own home! →

Image by
Kevin Low

Stanley Baxter

Many languages influence the language spoken today, and several languages have been spoken in the Glasgow area. The very name Glasgow – the dear green place – comes from the form of Welsh spoken in the Kingdom of Strathclyde around the tenth century. Little survives of that language except for a few place names. The same could be said of the Gaelic tongue which replaced it and dominated the area by the twelfth century. It in turn was superseded by the ancestor of the main component of the dialect spoken in Glasgow today, Scots.

Scots is descended from the northern form of Old English, whereas Standard English is descended from the southern dialect of Old English. Ironically, Scots retains Old English sounds and words which have long since disappeared from the Standard English of England. Thus if an Old English-speaking Anglian prince could time-travel to the present, he would have great difficulty communicating with the denizens of a Hampstead wine bar. In a Glasgow howff like the Sarry Heid, however, nae borra! Like the prince, Glaswegians say hoose and doon rather than house and down, richt and nicht rather than right and night and they greet when reek gets in their een, rather than cry when smoke gets in their eyes! Knowing Glasgow's openness to strangers, your prince would not only understand every word spoken in the Sarry Heid, he would have a rerr terr as well: 'By ra way, see ra next time some wee English nyaff wi bools in his mooth tells me Ah talk garbage, Hrothgar, Ah'll gie 'm laldy aboot you an aw thay Anglian princes talkin' like me n'that – here's tae us, wee man, wha's like us, cheers!!'

Although from Old English roots, by the 1400s Scots felt their language had become so different from the sister language to the South, that what had been known as 'Inglis', from then on was called 'Scots'. English and Scots were like Dutch and German or Spanish and Portuguese, languages from the same roots which developed differently due to their belonging to separate political entities. French, Scandinavian, Dutch, Gaelic and Latin all influenced Scots and by the fifteenth and sixteenth centuries it was a wonderfully flexible medium for poets and princes, lawyers and laymen.

Glasgow folk speak the west central dialect of Scots, saying for example baw, snaw and awaw,

while a Scots speaker further to the north-east would say baa, snaa and awa. The same original dialect is spoken in Glasgow's hinterland in the industrial towns and farming areas of Lanarkshire, Renfrewshire and Ayrshire. It was also the main dialect of Scots to go with the settlers to Northern Ireland in the seventeenth century, and is still spoken vigorously in County Antrim and County Down – one of the reasons for the strong rapport between the Scots and Irish.

In the nineteenth century there flocked to Glasgow Gaelic Highlanders, Irish peasants, east European Jews, Italians and lowland Scots speaking every dialect from Ecclefechan to Orkney. The lingua franca that emerged into the Glasgow dialect was still recognizably Scots, but with some of the features of the dialect spoken a few miles outwith the city planed away. Thus an Ayrshireman like me would say ye ken, seiven, and brocht, while a Glaswegian would say ye know, seven, and brought.

But if there were some losses when the differences were smoothed away for ease of communication, there were also gains as the locals adopted expressions from the incomers. The old derogatory term for a cornerboy, the Glesga keelie, comes from the Gaelic gille (boy). And though his origin is obscure, the rotund personage celebrated in Glasgow humour as the wee bauchle, may have started his life as a buachaill – a cow-boy in Irish Gaelic.

No panoply of Glasgow characters would be complete without the diminutive person of stunted growth, the wee nyaff. That comes from the native Scots dialect, as does the adjective which adds to the nyaffs attractiveness, shuilpit (drawn, sickly) – the shuilpit wee nyaff. The huge Irish immigrant population influenced the dialect in other ways – that essential plural missing in English and Scots youz – used in phrases like 'whaur i youz yins gaun?' – probably came from Irish English.

A curious phenomenon in language is that what starts as being identified with people at the lowest end of the social scale often percolates up through society. In the United States this has happened with black slang. In Britain the once dreaded glottal stop, associated with the urban masses who follow teams like the Glasgow Celtic, is now widespread in pukkah circles in English society. Listen to the young royals, for example, the next time they mention holidays in Scotland.

The reason for this upward percolation, I think, is because the language of the street has a vigour, directness and power missing in the more urbane, but bland utterings of the middle and upper classes. What better describes the pangs of hunger, for example, than the memorable Glasgow expression, 'Ah'm that hungry, Ah could eat a scabby heidit wean'.

Everyone has their own favourite example of cutting Glasgow humour and mine is a classic of the put down! Two cleaning ladies in the BBC in Glasgow were arguing hammer and tong, each drawing from the vast range of Scots invective: ya chancer, chantie wrastler, scunner, sumph, gomeril, eejit, heidbanger and so on, but eventually one lady came up with the one to which there was no reply, 'Hey, whit'll you dae fur a face, when King Kong asks for his erse back?'

There's a lot more to the Glasgow dialect than humour, for it is also a medium for innovative novels, poetry and powerful drama. For politicians, trade union leaders and punters who can exploit the full potential of both Standard English and the dialect, their speech is invested with a demotic power which is extremely convincing. Because of this, and its frequent use on radio and television, it is a language which is travelling well beyond the city and influencing the local speech in places as far apart as Langholm and Lerwick.

The society for the Queen's English may recoil in horrid fascination from expressions like 'ah'm ur not' (I am not) or 'ah'm ur sot' (I am so), Scots language purists may greet over young Glaswegians inability to pronounce the guttural ch sound – Docherty is now Dockerty – but Glasgow goes its own way, now confident enough in its speech to ignore both sides. Given the weight of sheer numbers – forty per cent of the population of Scotland live in and around Glasgow, Glasgow will continue to exercise a tremendous influence over Scottish speech. It is very much the language of the future. The language, even, of 1990.

Rachel Meehan

'The Kilpatrick Fort was made large, capable of holding a full cohort and was protected by triple rows of ramparts and ditches. The hamlet of Kilpatrick and many of the adjoining field dykes were built from the ruins. About two years ago the last vestiges of this ancient stronghold, fraught with many interesting historical associations, were ruthlessly removed to make room for a cluster of villas, with the uncouth appellation of "Bearsden".'

(The Lennox, 1874.)

DECEMBER

The Big Noise

JAN TO DEC

CITY WIDE

Don't let the year pass without catching some of the feast of theatre, sports, visual arts, storytelling and just about everything else you can think of which is launched with **Blast Off**, the opening event in the 1990 celebration of youth. From tots to teens, there will be something for everyone and all of it reported in the new young peoples' newspaper, Cult. Hordes of professional actors, directors and artists have collaborated with young people of all ages and all parts of the City in one of the most exciting events of the year.

People's Palace

1 JAN TO 31 DEC

Throughout the year, the People's Palace will run a series of exhibitions of the popular arts and crafts, for which they are rightly famous. These will range from **The Fabric of Glasgow** – a display of banners made in the east end to a review of cake icing – one of the butterfly arts, brilliant and shortlived. Don't miss **A Rerr Terr Arraferr** – a celebration of the traditional Glasgow Fair.

HOW TO BOOK

Main Box Office:
The Ticket Centre
Candleriggs
Glasgow G1 1NQ.

Open: Monday to Saturday 10.30 - 6.30 p.m.
Tel: 041 227 5511.

Booking by phone available to Access, Visa, Style, American Express. Credit card bookings also available by post.

Tickets are also available from individual venues. (See local press for details)

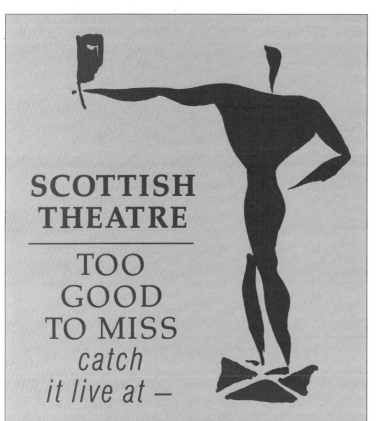

HEATHER CREAM

— Liqueur —

A luxurious
flavour
of Scotland

Pure
malt whisky
blended
with fresh
scottish
cream

*

INVER HOUSE DISTILLERS LIMITED, AIRDRIE, LANARKSHIRE ML6 8PL, SCOTLAND
TELEPHONE: 0236 69377   TELEX: 778084   FAX: 0236 69781

WANTED in 30 countries around the world.

Hardly surprising with his record. TAGGART, the detective thriller serial and TAGGART THE MOVIE have always earned arresting ratings. On his home patch, throughout the United Kingdom's ITV network and in 30 other countries.

Yet our streetwise cop is just one character in the case of the television company that knows no frontiers.

Further evidence can be found in the sheer range of programmes made by Scottish Television. No other British ITV company makes more sports, religious, local entertainment and local politics programmes than we do.

WHO EXPOSED MRS. MACK?

Scottish is the only regional company to create a drama serial which the entire network buys – TAKE THE HIGH ROAD. In all, we have sold over £15 million worth of programmes to the ITV network for 1990. (Surely even Mrs. Mack would admire our enterprise?)

PROGRAMME POWER

Another coup is THE DISNEY CLUB, the result of a dynamic initiative taken with the Disney Organisation. That relationship has also yielded the British rights to WIN, LOSE OR DRAW, the popular game show.

Scottish is also moving into feature films with KILLING DAD, starring Denholm Elliot and Julie Walters. We also co-funded THE BIG MAN starring Liam Neeson, Joanne Whalley-Kilmer and Billy Connolly.

THE ASTRONAUT CONNECTION

When the exclusive TV rights to the Juno Space Mission became available, it was Scottish Television who won them for ITV. The mission will put Britain's first astronaut into space and Scottish Television will be there every step of the way.

ALL CLUED UP

Technically, we are as clued up as anyone can be. The first simultaneous transmission to the Soviet Union, Eastern Europe and Western Europe was achieved by Scottish. And a recent £6 million investment in new technology means that our Glasgow and Edinburgh studios run with the most sophisticated equipment.

All of which leads us to an inescapable conclusion: Scottish is the one to watch.

SCOTTISH TELEVISION

AIR 2000

Growing from Glasgow

BUREAU DE CHANGE

FULL BANKING FACILITIES

90 St. Vincent Street, Glasgow. G2 5UQ Tel: 041 221 9585

YOU'RE BETTER OFF TALKING TO BARCLAYS

DISCOVER THE MOST EXCITING DEVELOPMENT TO COME TO TAYSIDE.

It's Dundee's Discovery Quay and, when it opens in 1991, it promises to be at the top of the tourist list in Scotland. There's so much for the whole family to see and do.

Budding sailors can visit Captain Scott's ship — RRS Discovery — walk the decks that he walked and see how the sailors lived during the voyage.

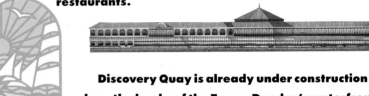

Discover all that's best in Dundee's glowing past and present at Discovery Quay's Heritage Centre.

Browse through the shopping mall or relax in one of the cafes or restaurants.

There are leisure facilities too for the more energetic. Dundee couldn't be better located. The city is on the major tourist routes North and just an hour's drive from Edinburgh and an hour and a half from Glasgow.

Discovery Quay is already under construction along the banks of the Tay on Dundee's waterfront and is due to open in the spring of 1991.

For further details telephone 0382 29122.

RENFREW DISTRICT

YOUR VISIT   ## OUR VISION

Renfrew District is on the doorstep of the cultural capital of Europe. It is an area simply bursting with historical and leisure attractions. The District boasts many fine golf courses, sailing at Lochwinnoch or swimming in one of the many leisure pools. The majestic Paisley Abbey sits proudly in the main town and the delights of Formakin Estate situated in beautiful countryside are but two of the many places of interest to visit.

For full details of everything there is to see and do contact.

Renfrew District is the fourth biggest in Scotland with a major international airport on its doorstep. It is an ideal location for business. The Renfrew Development Company is spearheading the Paisley and Renfrew initiative. Paisley International is its flagship project which will see the largest town in the district undergo major changes which will develop the whole area to its full potential. Two of the major visitor attractions this year will be the staging of an International Organ Festival and an International Colour Slide Exhibition.

For full details of all events and business opportunities contact.

Renfrew
DISTRICT COUNCIL

Renfrew District Council
Department of Planning & Development
Municipal Buildings
Cotton Street Paisley PA1 1BU
Tel: 041-889 5400. Fax: 041-889 0361.

RENFREW DEVELOPMENT COMPANY
St. James Business Centre
Linwood Road, Paisley PA3 3AT
Tel: 041-887 5922. Fax: 041-889 9405.

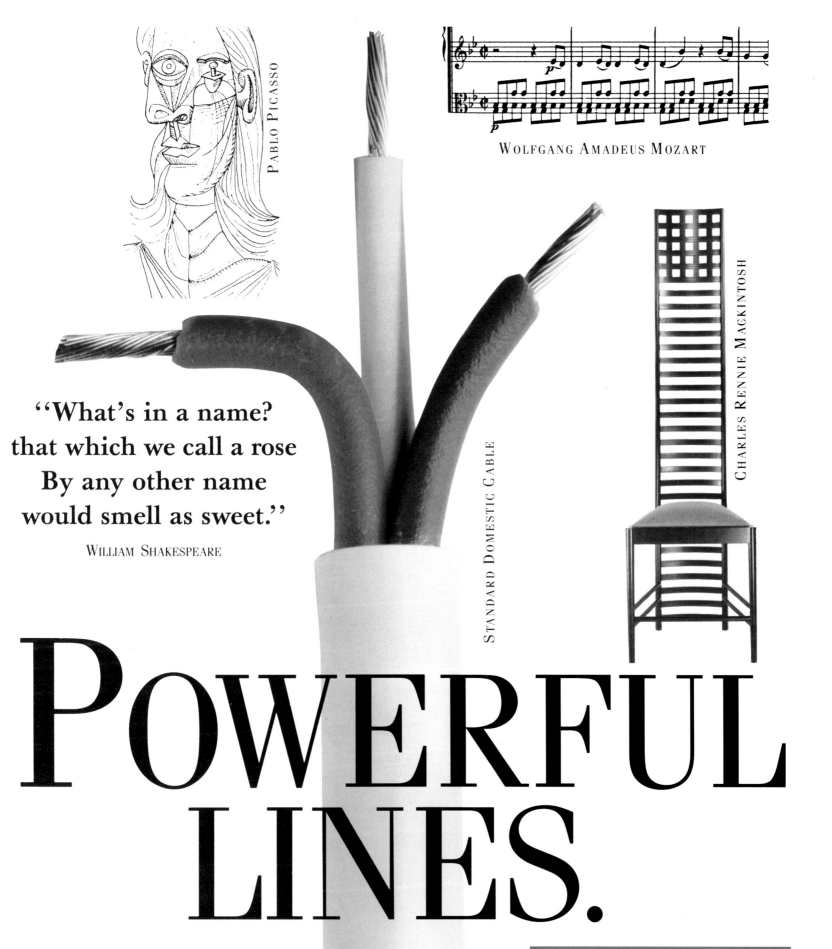

PABLO PICASSO

WOLFGANG AMADEUS MOZART

CHARLES RENNIE MACKINTOSH

STANDARD DOMESTIC CABLE

"What's in a name?
that which we call a rose
By any other name
would smell as sweet."

WILLIAM SHAKESPEARE

POWERFUL LINES.

Lines which inspire, intrigue and influence. Lines which give warmth, light
and energy. We are in favour of them all, as elements vital to modern life.

Scottish Power

Successor to the South of Scotland Electricity Board.

(R)EVOLUTIONARY JAZZ!
29th June - 8th July 1990

The 4th

GLASGOW
International
JAZZ FESTIVAL

For details contact:
Glasgow International Jazz Festival
46 Royal Exchange Square
GLASGOW G1 3AR

Telephone
041 226 3262

GLASGOW 1990
CULTURAL CAPITAL OF EUROPE

An integral part of Glasgow's celebrations as Cultural Capital of Europe 1990.

The biggest free distribution newspaper in Britain

Over 660,000* readers every week

...pure dead brilliant!

*Market Research Scotland readership survey Sept 1989

When you're in and around Glasgow, travel Strathclyde's 'Happy' Buses. Just like Glaswegians do. 136 million times a year.

Strathclyde's Buses

Travel happy.

THE BROOMIELAW – GLASGOW'S WATERFRONT TO THE WORLD

Glasgow's great prosperity during the 19th Century was founded on the city's pre-eminence as a port. Yet, in 1775 the River Clyde was a mere 16 inches deep until far-sighted merchants had it dredged right into the heart of the city – to The Broomielaw, the principal quay in what was then "The Second City of the Empire".

Now, that same spirit of enterprise and far-sightedness which first made Glasgow great is stirring again along The Broomielaw.

In what is probably the largest project of its kind ever undertaken outside London, the nine acre Broomielaw site is being transformed. A new kind of commercial centre is being created to carry the legacy of The Broomielaw into the 1990s and beyond.

Valued at over £250 million, state-of-the-art HQ office buildings are being developed.

Due for completion in the early 90s, The Broomielaw will offer over one million square feet of prestigious office accommodation to national and international companies and organisations.

A new commercial centre is rising out of the old Broomielaw – Glasgow's Waterfront to the World.

THE BROOMIELAW
Glasgow's waterfront to the world

Glasgow & Oriental Developments Limited, 150 Broomielaw, Glasgow G1 4RE. Tel: 041-221 3976. Fax: 041-221 4926.

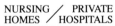
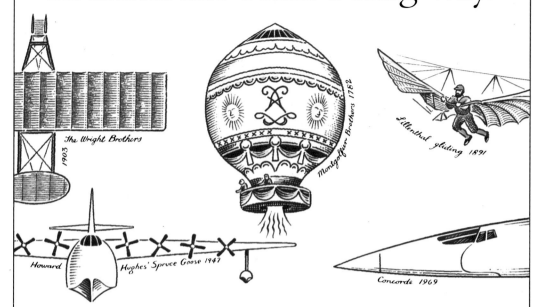

    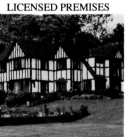

James Christie 1733-1803 painted by Thomas Gainsborough.
James Christie was born in Perth, Scotland and founded Christie's,
the international fine art auction house, in 1766.

Encouraging the future
Appreciating the past

For further information on Christie's exhibitions during the Year of
Culture and forthcoming sales please write to the Public Relations
Office in Glasgow

164-166 Bath Street
Glasgow G2 4TG
Telephone 041-332 8134

CHRISTIE'S

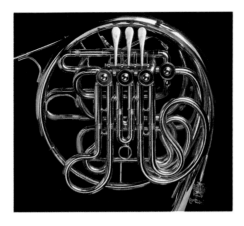

GLASGOW 1990
CULTURAL CAPITAL OF EUROPE

We're right behind you.

THE HEART AND SOUL OF 1990!
AN EXPERIENCE YOU'LL NEVER FORGET.

GLASGOW'S *glasgow* **A CITY WITHIN A CITY**

Glasgow's Glasgow is a breath-taking and dramatic experience and an ever-changing programme of entertainment events rolled into one. All under one roof, in 22 vaulted arches under Central Station. Years of detailed research have gone into producing this celebration of our great city.

But this is not simply an exhibition which you walk round and look at — you actually become a living part of it as you are swept into a vivid creation of the sights and sounds of Glasgow past and present.

Emigrate on a boat to Canada; explore a Glasgow tenement; use a periscope in Great Western Road and meet Lord Kelvin; join the UCS work-in; vote on the Act of Union; ride the first-ever bicycle; watch Scotland's finest World Cup goals and see Benny Lynch in his prime.

Admire over 1500 treasures from all over the world, from the V & A, from the Science Museum and the Palace of Westminster. 3 live promenade theatre performances a day bring Glasgow's past to life whilst audio-visual displays and 40 sound cones tell their own stories.

And after the exhibition closes at 8pm, The Arches Theatre, concert and cabaret scene jump to life every night till late, in a festive club atmosphere in the cafe, bar, restaurant and theatre.

There's something for everyone, young or old, Glaswegian or visitor. Don't miss it!

Glasgow's Glasgow. Midland Street. 7 days a week, April till November, 1990.

SCOTTISH METROPOLITAN

The Royal Exchange as viewed from Scottish Metropolitan's headquarters.

A SURE FOUNDATION ...

Scottish Metropolitan is an established property investment and development company with its roots firmly in Glasgow.

From its base in the City of Culture, the Company is spreading its tradition for quality throughout the UK.

It is this quality which underlines Scottish Metropolitan's pride in its numerous contributions to the conservation of the City's heritage and the preservation of its culture.

... FOR A POSITIVE FUTURE

Royal Exchange House, 100 Queen Street, Glasgow G1 3DL. 041-248 7333.

'The Class' by Robert Heindel.

Esprit de Corps

The Scottish Ballet

There's always something happening at Princes Square

Princes Square occupies a beautifully restored listed building dating from 1841 which is now Scotland's finest speciality shopping centre. The renaissance of Glasgow has been widely recognised and Princes Square captures the essence of the city's enhanced image.

Entering from Buchanan Street, visitors can revel in the array of highly individual shops plus themed wine bars, cafes and restaurants. The choice, variety and sheer delight of discovering over 60 shops unmatched for style, quality and service under an attractive domed roof makes a visit to Princes Square a "must".

You can browse through five levels of fashion, accessories, leather goods, books, handcrafted designer jewellery, specialist gift boutiques

with Scottish hand crafted goods available from original craftcarts. Relax over a freshly brewed coffee and enjoy a variety of entertainment regularly scheduled for Thursday and Sunday afternoons with special events arranged almost daily.

Princes Square shops and the Terraced Foodcourts are open 10.00am-7.00pm Monday to Saturday, 11.00am to 5.00pm Sunday.

The licensed restaurants are open from 11am until midnight.

PRINCES SQUARE SHOPPING 48 BUCHANAN ST GLASGOW
THE DIFFERENCE IS DAY AND NIGHT

2.75
MILLION

The Daily Record and Sunday Mail reaches more people in Scotland than any other newspapers put together.
Over 2,750,000 Adult Readers – that's almost 70%.
So, whoever you want to reach, wherever they are in Scotland, why take less than The Best?

SCOTLAND'S BEST

THERE IS NO ALTERNATIVE

To advertise in the Daily Record & Sunday Mail contact
Gordon B. Terris on 041-242 3451.

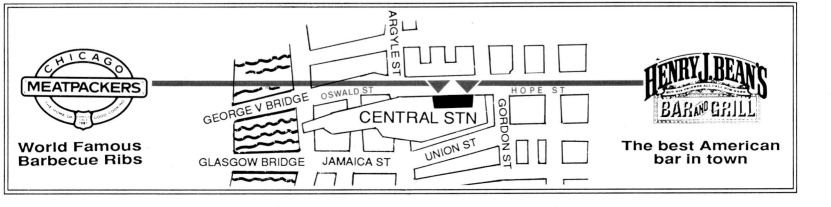

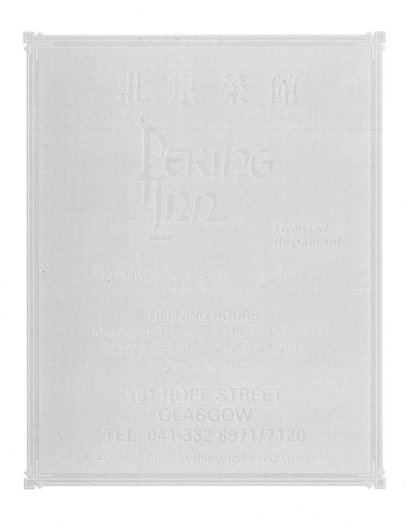

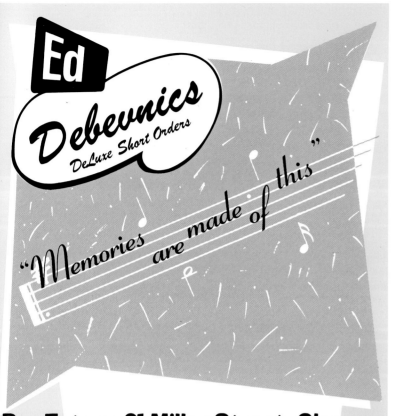

Andy Ewan

Sarah Allen and sister

Michelle T

Michael Ross

Laurina He

Barry Wright

Michael W Rus

The Book – Glasgow 1990
was project managed by
Network Scotland Ltd,
The Mews, 57 Ruthven
Lane, Glasgow on behalf
of The Festivals Unit,
Glasgow District Council
and designed by
The Yellow Pencil Company,
2 Cosser St, London
SE1 7BU.

Commissioning Editor:
The Festivals Office

Executive Editor:
Michael W Russell

Art Director
Andy Ewan

Editor:
Angus Stewart

Associate Editors:
Chris Dolan
Michelle Thomas

Designers
Sarah Allen
Michael Ross
SteMo

Project Co-ordinator:
Sandra Hatley

Research, Administration
& Secretarial:
Laurina Hewson
Karen Craig
Lucy Eadie
Carolyn Howieson
Ian Black
Jim Waugh

Advertising:
Simon Turner

Advertising Sales:
Gina Ireland
Contact Publicity

cultural capital of europe

In 1985 the European Ministers of Culture decided to make a special award each year to one city in Europe. The chosen city would hold the title of Cultural Capital of Europe for one year and be asked to mark the accolade in ways which could demonstrate particular aspects of the city's culture to the rest of Europe.

The first city chosen was Athens in 1985. Florence (1986), Amsterdam (1987), Berlin (1988) and Paris (1989) have also received the title. Dublin will be the Cultural Capital of Europe in 1991.

The United Kingdom was invited to nominate one of its cities for 1990. The Minister for the Arts approached local authorities in England, Wales and Scotland for nominations. The final UK shortlist included two Scottish cities – Edinburgh and Glasgow. The shortlist also included two Welsh cities – Cardiff and Swansea, and five English cities – Bath, Bristol, Cambridge, Leeds and Liverpool.

Each of the cities was invited to compete for the prize. Glasgow's submission was confident and clear: it drew attention to the cities remarkable history, to its cultural facilities and institutions, to its organizational structures and personalities and to its ability to develop a special programme building on past successes.

With the support of all political parties, and co-operation between public and private sectors, Glasgow argued its corner. It boasted it was *already* a European cultural capital. The Minister agreed. Late in 1986 Richard Luce, as Minister for the Arts announced that Glasgow would be Britain's nomination for Cultural Capital of Europe in 1990. His nomination was unanimously approved by the European Ministers of Culture.

Glasgow 1990 had begun...

Angus Stewart

Sandra Hatley

First published 1990

Copyright © 1990, Glasgow
District Council

ISBN 0 00 435662-4
Published by **William Collins
and Sons Co Ltd** in conjunction
with **Network Scotland Ltd** an
Glasgow District Council.

Distributed by **William Collins
Sons and Co Ltd**, PO Box
Glasgow G4 0NB

Printed by **Waddies Web
Division**, Deans Industrial
Estate, Livingston, Scotland.
Typesetting by
Midford Typesetting Ltd.
Colour Separation by
Pegasus.

SteMo

Chris Dolan

The Glenlivet.®
Scotland's first malt whisky.

'...and now for 1991!'

On the 1st of January 1991 Dublin becomes the Cultural
Capital of Europe.
What will last from Glasgow's reign? The place and the
people will carry on. How will they be changed?

The tangible legacies will include the Glasgow International Concert Hall
– the venue for Glasgow for many years to come. The MacLellan Galleries,
the Tramway, and many other Glasgow buildings will continue into the last
decade of the twentieth century revitalized. The city will be the richer.

But buildings without people are empty shells. Glasgow was the 'second
city of the empire'. But by the 1960s Glasgow was viewed from outside as
dirty, hostile and unappealing. For many young Glaswegians the only way
to 'get on' was to 'get out'.

The 1980s have been the decade of resurgence. New building, and
sensitive (and sensible) restoration have transformed the heart of the city.
People have found new outlets for their creative talents that have
produced new employment and new economic opportunities. The Garden
Festival of 1988 restored the image of green to our 'dear green place'. The
events of 1990 will have started a new decade by voicing optimism and
confidence.

Hundreds of thousands of those who live in Glasgow will have taken part
in, visited, looked at, listened to, or heard about events that brought
excitement to their lives. The buildings they have happened in, or around,
were part of the landscape: the meaning may have touched a chord that
resonates long after 1990. And collectively Glasgow, in its depreciating
way, may again be able to say that it is 'no mean city'.

Cailean Russell
Here is the future

For Glasgow has been Cultural Capital of Europe. A swan has broken out
of the ugly feathers of its recent past and is learning to fly. There are still
problems to be solved: peripheral housing to be given a human aspect:
deprivation to be relieved: jobs to be created. A future without problems is
not an earthly, let alone a Scottish future.

But 1990 was part of a process. In the January smirr of 1991 there will be a
new spirit abroad. A spirit of a city that is back where it belongs!